Working Papers: Chapters 1–17

Accounting, 27e and Financial Accounting, 15e

Carl S. Warren
Professor Emeritus of Accounting
University of Georgia, Athens

James M. Reeve
Professor Emeritus of Accounting
University of Tennessee, Knoxville

Jonathan E. Duchac
Professor of Accounting
Wake Forest University

CENGAGE Learning

Australia • Brazil • Mexico • Singapore • United Kingdom • United States

CENGAGE
Learning

For product information and technology assistance, contact us at **Cengage Learning Customer & Sales Support, 1-800-354-9706**.

For permission to use material from this text or product, submit all requests online at **www.cengage.com/permissions**
Further permissions questions can be emailed to **permissionrequest@cengage.com**.

ISBN: 978-1-337-27215-5

Cengage Learning
20 Channel Center Street
Boston, MA 02210
USA

Cengage Learning is a leading provider of customized learning solutions with office locations around the globe, including Singapore, the United Kingdom, Australia, Mexico, Brazil, and Japan. Locate your local office at: **www.cengage.com/global**.

Cengage Learning products are represented in Canada by Nelson Education, Ltd.

To learn more about Cengage Learning Solutions, visit **www.cengage.com**.

Purchase any of our products at your local college store or at our preferred online store **www.cengagebrain.com**.

Printed in the United States of America
2 3 4 5 6 21 20 19 18 17

CONTENTS

PREFACE

The working papers include problem-specific forms for preparing solutions for Exercises, A&B Problems, the Continuing Problem, and the Comprehensive Problems from the textbook. These forms, with preprinted headings, provide a structure for the problems, which will help you get started and save you time.

Based on students' testimonials and instructors' feedback, the forms in the working papers have been streamlined to make them simpler to use and to better reflect the changing environment of business. For example, the vertical rules that separated digits of numbers entered into journals, ledgers, and statements have been removed, making it easier to write in numbers.

Note that when entering whole amounts into the forms, your instructor will direct you on whether to include a decimal point and zeroes (e.g., 100.00) or to omit those (e.g., 100).

Name ______________________________

EXERCISE 1-1

a. 1. ____________ 6. ____________ 11. ____________
2. ____________ 7. ____________ 12. ____________
3. ____________ 8. ____________ 13. ____________
4. ____________ 9. ____________ 14. ____________
5. ____________ 10. ____________ 15. ____________

b. ______________________________

EXERCISE 1-2

____

EXERCISE 1-3

a. 1. ____________ 6. ____________
2. ____________ 7. ____________
3. ____________ 8. ____________
4. ____________ 9. ____________
5. ____________ 10. ____________

b. ______________________________

EXERCISE 1-4

____

EXERCISE 1-5

____

EXERCISE 1-6

	Assets	=	Liabilities	+	Owner's Equity
a.	________	=	$556,000	+	$3,374,000
b.	$6,111,200	=	________	+	$5,725,000
c.	$2,150,000	=	$812,500	+	________

EXERCISE 1-7

a. ______________________

b. ______________________

c. ______________________

d. ______________________

e. ______________________

EXERCISE 1-8

a. ______________________

b. ______________________

c. ______________________

d. ______________________

e. ______________________

f. ______________________

g. ______________________

EXERCISE 1-9

a. ______________________

b. ______________________

c. ______________________

d. ______________________

e. ______________________

EXERCISE 1-10

a. (1) Assets: ______________________

(2) Liabilities: ______________________

(3) Owner's equity: ______________________

b. (1) Assets: ______________________

(2) Liabilities: ______________________

(3) Owner's equity: ______________________

Name ______________________________

EXERCISE 1-10, Concluded

c. ______________________________

____

____

____

____

EXERCISE 1-11

1. Expenses: ______________________________
2. Owner's investments: ______________________________
3. Owner's withdrawals: ______________________________
4. Revenues: ______________________________

EXERCISE 1-12

1. ______________________________
2. ______________________________
3. ______________________________
4. ______________________________
5. ______________________________
6. ______________________________
7. ______________________________
8. ______________________________
9. ______________________________
10. ______________________________

EXERCISE 1-13

a. (1) ______________________________
(2) ______________________________
(3) ______________________________
(4) ______________________________
(5) ______________________________
(6) ______________________________
(7) ______________________________
b. ______________________________
c. ______________________________
d. ______________________________
e. ______________________________

EXERCISE 1-14

____

____

____

____

EXERCISE 1-15

Jupiter:

Mars:

Saturn:

Venus:

Name ______________________________

EXERCISE 1-16

1. Accounts Payable: ______________________________
2. Accounts Receivable: ______________________________
3. Andrew King, Capital: ______________________________
4. Cash: ______________________________
5. Fees Earned: ______________________________
6. Land: ______________________________
7. Rent Expense: ______________________________
8. Supplies: ______________________________
9. Wages Expense: ______________________________
10. Wages Payable: ______________________________

EXERCISE 1-17

1. Accounts Payable: ______________________________
2. Accounts Receivable: ______________________________
3. Andrew King, Capital: ______________________________
4. Cash: ______________________________
5. Fees Earned: ______________________________
6. Land: ______________________________
7. Rent Expense: ______________________________
8. Supplies: ______________________________
9. Wages Expense: ______________________________
10. Wages Payable: ______________________________

EXERCISE 1-18

a.

Statement of Owner's Equity

EXERCISE 1-18, Concluded

b. ____

EXERCISE 1-19

Income Statement

Name ______________________________

EXERCISE 1-20

Freeman:

Heyward:

Jones:

Ramirez:

EXERCISE 1-21

a.

Balance Sheet

Balance Sheet

EXERCISE 1-21, Concluded

b.		
c.		

EXERCISE 1-22

a. 1. Accounts payable: ______
2. Cash equivalents: ______
3. Crude oil inventory: ______
4. Equipment: ______
5. Exploration expenses: ______
6. Income taxes payable: ______
7. Investments: ______
8. Long-term debt: ______
9. Marketable securities: ______
10. Notes and loans payable: ______
11. Notes receivable: ______
12. Operating expenses: ______
13. Prepaid taxes: ______
14. Sales: ______
15. Selling expenses: ______

EXERCISE 1-22, Concluded

b. ______________________

c. ______________________

EXERCISE 1-23

1. Cash received from fees earned: ______________________
2. Cash paid for expenses: ______________________
3. Cash paid for land: ______________________
4. Cash paid to owner for personal use: ______________________

EXERCISE 1-24

Statement of Cash Flows

Name ________________________________

EXERCISE 1-25

EXERCISE 1-25, Continued

(Optional)

Income Statement

Statement of Owner's Equity

EXERCISE 1-25, Concluded

(Optional)

Balance Sheet

EXERCISE 1-26

a. ____

____

b. ____

____

c. ____

____

____

EXERCISE 1-27

a. ____

____

b. ____

____

c. ____

____

d. ____

____

____

____

____

____

____

____

PROBLEM 1-1 ___

1.

	Assets			= Liabilities +	Owner's Equity							
	Cash +	Accounts Receivable +	Supplies =	Accounts Payable +	____, Capital –	____, Drawing +	Fees Earned –	Rent Exp. –	Sal. Exp. –	Supp. Exp. –	Auto Exp. –	Misc. Exp.
a.												
b.												
Bal.												
c.												
Bal.												
d.												
Bal.												
e.												
Bal.												
f.												
Bal.												
g.												
Bal.												
h.												
Bal.												
i.												
Bal.												
j.												
Bal.												

PROBLEM 1-1 ___, Concluded

2. ______________________________

3. ______________________________

4. ______________________________

Name ______________________________

PROBLEM 1-2 ___

1.

Income Statement

2.

Statement of Owner's Equity

PROBLEM 1-2 ___, Concluded

3.

____

Balance Sheet

____

4. ____

____

Name ______________________________

PROBLEM 1-3 ___

1.

Income Statement

2.

Statement of Owner's Equity

PROBLEM 1-3 ___, Concluded

3.

Balance Sheet

4. (Optional)

Statement of Cash Flows

PROBLEM 1-4 ___

1.

	Assets		Liabilities	Owner's Equity							
	Cash	+ Supplies	= Accounts Payable	+ ________, Capital	– ________, Drawing	+ Sales Comm.	– Rent Exp.	– Sal. Exp.	– Auto Exp.	– Supp. Exp.	– Misc. Exp.
a.											
b.											
Bal.											
c.											
Bal.											
d.											
Bal.											
e.											
Bal.											
f.											
Bal.											
g.											
Bal.											
h.											
Bal.											
i.											
Bal.											

PROBLEM 1-4 ___, Continued

2.

Income Statement

Statement of Owner's Equity

PROBLEM 1-4 ___, Concluded

Balance Sheet

This Page Not Used.

PROBLEM 1-5 ___

1.

ASSETS							=	LIABILITIES	+	OWNER'S EQUITY
Cash	+	Accounts Receivable	+	Supplies	+	Land	=	Accounts Payable	+	________, Capital
________	+	________	+	________	+	________	=	________	+	________, Capital
________							=	________	+	________, Capital
________							=	________, Capital		

PROBLEM 1-5 ___, Continued

2.

	ASSETS				= LIABILITIES +	OWNER'S EQUITY									
	Cash	+ Accts. Rec.	+ Supplies	+ Land	= Accts. Payable	+ ______, Capital	– ______, Drawing	+ Dry Cleaning Revenue	– Dry Cleaning Exp.	– Wages Exp.	– Rent Exp.	– Supp. Exp.	– Truck Exp.	– Util. Exp.	– Misc. Exp.
Bal.															
a.															
Bal.															
b.															
Bal.															
c.															
Bal.															
d.															
Bal.															
e.															
Bal.															
f.															
Bal.															
g.															
Bal.															
h.															
Bal.															
i.															
Bal.															
j.															
Bal.															
k.															
Bal.															
l.															
Bal.															

PROBLEM 1-5 ___, Continued

3.

Income Statement

Statement of Owner's Equity

PROBLEM 1-5 ___, Continued

Balance Sheet

PROBLEM 1-5 ___, Concluded

4. (Optional)

Statement of Cash Flows

This Page Not Used.

Name ______________________________

PROBLEM 1-6 ___

a. ______________________________

____

b. ______________________________

____

c. ______________________________

____

d. ______________________________

____

e. ______________________________

____

f. ______________________________

____

g. ______________________________

____

h. ______________________________

____

i. ______________________________

____

j. ______________________________

____

____

k. ______________________________

____

l. ______________________________

____

m. ______________________________

____

____

n. ______________________________

____

o. ______________________________

____

p. ______________________________

____

____

This Page Not Used.

CONTINUING PROBLEM

1.

	ASSETS			= LIABILITIES +	OWNER'S EQUITY										
	Cash +	Accts. Rec. +	Supplies =	Accts. Pay. +	Peyton Smith, Capital –	Peyton Smith, Drawing +	Fees Earned –	Music Exp. –	Office Rent Exp. –	Equip. Rent Exp. –	Adv. Exp. –	Wages Exp. –	Util. Exp. –	Sup. Exp. –	Misc. Exp.
6/1															
6/2															
Bal.															
6/2															
Bal.															
6/4															
Bal.															
6/6															
Bal.															
6/8															
Bal.															
6/12															
Bal.															
6/13															
Bal.															
6/16															
Bal.															
6/22															
Bal.															
6/25															
Bal.															

CONTINUING PROBLEM, Continued

	Assets			= Liabilities +	Owner's Equity											
	Cash +	Accts. Rec. +	Supplies =	Accts. Pay. +	Peyton Smith, Capital –	Peyton Smith, Drawing +	Fees Earned –	Music Exp. –	Office Rent Exp. –	Equip. Rent Exp. –	Adv. Exp. –	Wages Exp. –	Util. Exp. –	Sup. Exp. –	Misc. Exp.
6/29															
Bal.															
6/30															
Bal.															
6/30															
Bal.															
6/30															
Bal.															
6/30															
Bal.															
6/30															
Bal.															
6/30															
Bal.															
6/30															
Bal.															

Name ____________________

CONTINUING PROBLEM, Continued

2.

Income Statement

3.

Statement of Owner's Equity

CONTINUING PROBLEM, Concluded

4.

Balance Sheet

Name ______________________________

EXERCISE 2-1

Accounts Payable: ______________________________

Advanced Payments for Equipment: ______________________________

Air Traffic Liability: ______________________________

Aircraft Fuel (Expense): ______________________________

Aircraft Maintenance (Expense): ______________________________

Aircraft Rent (Expense): ______________________________

Cargo Revenue: ______________________________

Cash: ______________________________

Contract Carrier Arrangements (Expense): ______________________________

Flight Equipment: ______________________________

Frequent Flyer (Obligations): ______________________________

Fuel Inventory: ______________________________

Landing Fees (Expense): ______________________________

Parts and Supplies: ______________________________

Passenger Commissions (Expense): ______________________________

Passenger Revenue: ______________________________

Prepaid Expenses: ______________________________

Taxes Payable: ______________________________

EXERCISE 2-2

Account	Account Number
Accounts Payable.................	________
Accounts Receivable............	________
Cash	________
Fees Earned..........................	________
Fred Biggs, Capital................	________
Fred Biggs, Drawing.............	________
Land	________
Miscellaneous Expense	________
Supplies Expense	________
Wages Expense	________

EXERCISE 2-3

Balance Sheet Accounts

Acct. #	Account Name
	1. Assets
	2. Liabilities
	3. Owner's Equity

Income Statement Accounts

Acct. #	Account Name
	4. Revenue
	5. Expenses

EXERCISE 2-4

	Increase	Decrease	Normal Balance
Balance sheet accounts:			
Asset	(a) ____	(b) ____	(c) ____
Liability	(d) ____	Debit	(e) ____
Owner's Equity:			
Capital	Credit	(f) ____	Credit
Drawing	(g) ____	(h) ____	(i) ____
Income statement accounts:			
Revenue	(j) ____	(k) ____	Credit
Expense	(l) ____	Credit	Debit

Name ____________________________________

EXERCISE 2-5

1. Accounts Payable: ____________________
2. Accounts Receivable: ____________________
3. Cash: ____________________
4. Fees Earned: ____________________
5. Insurance Expense: ____________________
6. Jerri Holt, Drawing: ____________________
7. Utilities Expense: ____________________

EXERCISE 2-6

a. Accounts Payable: ____________________
b. Accounts Receivable: ____________________
c. Ashley Griffin, Capital: ____________________
d. Ashley Griffin, Drawing: ____________________
e. Cash: ____________________
f. Fees Earned: ____________________
g. Office Equipment: ____________________
h. Rent Expense: ____________________
i. Supplies: ____________________
j. Wages Expense: ____________________

EXERCISE 2-7

JOURNAL

PAGE

	DATE		DESCRIPTION	POST. REF.	DEBIT	CREDIT	
1							1
2							2
3							3
4							4
5							5
6							6
7							7
8							8
9							9
10							10
11							11
12							12
13							13
14							14
15							15
16							16
17							17
18							18
19							19
20							20
21							21
22							22
23							23
24							24
25							25
26							26
27							27
28							28
29							29
30							30
31							31
32							32
33							33
34							34
35							35
36							36

Name ______________________________

EXERCISE 2-8

a.

JOURNAL

PAGE *87*

	DATE		DESCRIPTION	POST. REF.	DEBIT	CREDIT	
1							1
2							2
3							3
4							4
5							5
6							6

b., c., and d.

ACCOUNT ACCOUNT NO.

DATE		ITEM	POST. REF.	DEBIT	CREDIT	BALANCE	
						DEBIT	CREDIT

ACCOUNT ACCOUNT NO.

DATE		ITEM	POST. REF.	DEBIT	CREDIT	BALANCE	
						DEBIT	CREDIT

e. ______________________________

EXERCISE 2-9

a.

JOURNAL PAGE

	DATE		DESCRIPTION	POST. REF.	DEBIT	CREDIT	
1							1
2							2
3							3
4							4
5							5
6							6
7							7
8							8
9							9
10							10
11							11
12							12

b.

Cash

Accounts Payable

Supplies

Fees Earned

Accounts Receivable

c. ______________________

Name ______________________________

EXERCISE 2-10

a. ______________________________

b. ______________________________

EXERCISE 2-11

a.

Accounts Payable

b.

Accounts Receivable

EXERCISE 2-11, Concluded

c.

Cash

EXERCISE 2-12

a.

b.

EXERCISE 2-13

a. and b.

	Account Debited		Account Credited	
Transaction	**Type**	**Effect**	**Type**	**Effect**
(1)	asset	+	owner's equity	+
(2)				
(3)				
(4)				
(5)				
(6)				
(7)				
(8)				
(9)				

EXERCISE 2-14

JOURNAL

PAGE

DATE		DESCRIPTION	POST. REF.	DEBIT	CREDIT

Name ____________________________________

EXERCISE 2-15

a.

Unadjusted Trial Balance

b. ____

EXERCISE 2-16

Unadjusted Trial Balance

EXERCISE 2-17

Name ______________________________

EXERCISE 2-18

Unadjusted Trial Balance

EXERCISE 2-19

Error	(a) Out of Balance	(b) Difference	(c) Larger Total
1.	yes	$6,000	debit
2.			
3.			
4.			
5.			
6.			
7.			

EXERCISE 2-20

(Optional)

Unadjusted Trial Balance

Name ______________________________

EXERCISE 2-21

JOURNAL

PAGE ______

	DATE		DESCRIPTION	POST. REF.	DEBIT	CREDIT	
1							1
2							2
3							3
4							4
5							5
6							6
7							7
8							8
9							9

EXERCISE 2-22

JOURNAL

PAGE ______

	DATE		DESCRIPTION	POST. REF.	DEBIT	CREDIT	
1							1
2							2
3							3
4							4
5							5
6							6
7							7
8							8
9							9
10							10
11							11
12							12

EXERCISE 2-23

a. **1.** Revenue: ______________________________

____

2. Operating expenses: ______________________________

____

3. Operating income: ______________________________

____

EXERCISE 2-23, Concluded

b. ______________________

EXERCISE 2-24

a. 1. Revenue: ______________________

2. Operating expenses: ______________________

3. Operating income: ______________________

b. ______________________

c. ______________________

Name ______________________________

PROBLEM 2-1 ___

1. and 2.

Cash

Accounts Receivable

Supplies

Prepaid Insurance

Automobiles

PROBLEM 2-1 ___, Continued

Equipment

Accounts Payable

Notes Payable

______________, Capital

Professional Fees

Rent Expense

PROBLEM 2-1 ___, Continued

Salary Expense

Blueprint Expense

Automobile Expense

Miscellaneous Expense

PROBLEM 2-1 ___, Concluded

3.

Unadjusted Trial Balance

4. ____

____

Name ________________________________

PROBLEM 2-2 ___

1.

JOURNAL

PAGE

	DATE		DESCRIPTION	POST. REF.	DEBIT	CREDIT	
1							1
2							2
3							3
4							4
5							5
6							6
7							7
8							8
9							9
10							10
11							11
12							12
13							13
14							14
15							15
16							16
17							17
18							18
19							19
20							20
21							21
22							22
23							23
24							24
25							25
26							26
27							27
28							28
29							29
30							30
31							31
32							32
33							33
34							34
35							35

PROBLEM 2-2 ___, Continued

2.

Cash

Supplies

Accounts Payable

______________________, Capital

______________________, Drawing

Fees Earned

PROBLEM 2-2 ___, Continued

Rent Expense

Office Salaries Expense

Automobile Expense

Supplies Expense

Miscellaneous Expense

PROBLEM 2-2 ___, Concluded

3.

____

Unadjusted Trial Balance

____

4. a. ______________________________

b. ______________________________

c. ______________________________

5. ______________________________

____

Name ______________________________

PROBLEM 2-3 ___

1.

JOURNAL

PAGE 1

	DATE		DESCRIPTION	POST. REF.	DEBIT	CREDIT	
1							1
2							2
3							3
4							4
5							5
6							6
7							7
8							8
9							9
10							10
11							11
12							12
13							13
14							14
15							15
16							16
17							17
18							18
19							19
20							20
21							21
22							22
23							23
24							24
25							25
26							26
27							27
28							28
29							29
30							30
31							31
32							32
33							33
34							34
35							35

PROBLEM 2-3 ___, Continued

JOURNAL

PAGE 2

DATE		DESCRIPTION	POST. REF.	DEBIT	CREDIT

Name ______________________________

PROBLEM 2-3 ___, Continued

2.

GENERAL LEDGER

ACCOUNT *Cash* ACCOUNT NO. *11*

DATE		ITEM	POST. REF.	DEBIT	CREDIT	BALANCE DEBIT	BALANCE CREDIT

ACCOUNT *Accounts Receivable* ACCOUNT NO. *12*

DATE		ITEM	POST. REF.	DEBIT	CREDIT	BALANCE DEBIT	BALANCE CREDIT

ACCOUNT *Supplies* ACCOUNT NO. *13*

DATE		ITEM	POST. REF.	DEBIT	CREDIT	BALANCE DEBIT	BALANCE CREDIT

ACCOUNT *Prepaid Insurance* ACCOUNT NO. *14*

DATE		ITEM	POST. REF.	DEBIT	CREDIT	BALANCE DEBIT	BALANCE CREDIT

PROBLEM 2-3 ___, Continued

ACCOUNT *Equipment* ACCOUNT NO. *16*

DATE		ITEM	POST. REF.	DEBIT	CREDIT	BALANCE DEBIT	BALANCE CREDIT

ACCOUNT ACCOUNT NO. *18*

DATE		ITEM	POST. REF.	DEBIT	CREDIT	BALANCE DEBIT	BALANCE CREDIT

ACCOUNT *Notes Payable* ACCOUNT NO. *21*

DATE		ITEM	POST. REF.	DEBIT	CREDIT	BALANCE DEBIT	BALANCE CREDIT

ACCOUNT *Accounts Payable* ACCOUNT NO. *22*

DATE		ITEM	POST. REF.	DEBIT	CREDIT	BALANCE DEBIT	BALANCE CREDIT

ACCOUNT ______________________, *Capital* ACCOUNT NO. *31*

DATE		ITEM	POST. REF.	DEBIT	CREDIT	BALANCE DEBIT	BALANCE CREDIT

PROBLEM 2-3 ___, Continued

ACCOUNT ______________________, *Drawing* ACCOUNT NO. *32*

DATE		ITEM	POST. REF.	DEBIT	CREDIT	BALANCE DEBIT	BALANCE CREDIT

ACCOUNT *Fees Earned* ACCOUNT NO. *41*

DATE		ITEM	POST. REF.	DEBIT	CREDIT	BALANCE DEBIT	BALANCE CREDIT

ACCOUNT *Wages Expense* ACCOUNT NO. *51*

DATE		ITEM	POST. REF.	DEBIT	CREDIT	BALANCE DEBIT	BALANCE CREDIT

ACCOUNT *Rent Expense* ACCOUNT NO. *53*

DATE		ITEM	POST. REF.	DEBIT	CREDIT	BALANCE DEBIT	BALANCE CREDIT

ACCOUNT *Utilities Expense* ACCOUNT NO. *54*

DATE		ITEM	POST. REF.	DEBIT	CREDIT	BALANCE DEBIT	BALANCE CREDIT

PROBLEM 2-3 ___, Continued

ACCOUNT ACCOUNT NO. *55*

DATE		ITEM	POST. REF.	DEBIT	CREDIT	BALANCE	
						DEBIT	CREDIT

ACCOUNT *Miscellaneous Expense* ACCOUNT NO. *59*

DATE		ITEM	POST. REF.	DEBIT	CREDIT	BALANCE	
						DEBIT	CREDIT

PROBLEM 2-3 ___, Concluded

3.

Unadjusted Trial Balance

4. ______________________________

____

____

5. ______________________________

____

This Page Not Used.

Name ____________________

PROBLEM 2-4 ___

2. and 3.

JOURNAL

PAGE *18*

	DATE		DESCRIPTION	POST. REF.	DEBIT	CREDIT	
1							1
2							2
3							3
4							4
5							5
6							6
7							7
8							8
9							9
10							10
11							11
12							12
13							13
14							14
15							15
16							16
17							17
18							18
19							19
20							20
21							21
22							22
23							23
24							24
25							25
26							26
27							27
28							28
29							29
30							30
31							31
32							32
33							33
34							34
35							35

PROBLEM 2-4 ___, Continued

JOURNAL

PAGE 19

DATE		DESCRIPTION	POST. REF.	DEBIT	CREDIT

Name ___________________________

PROBLEM 2-4 ___, Continued

1. and 3.

GENERAL LEDGER

ACCOUNT *Cash* ACCOUNT NO. *11*

DATE		ITEM	POST. REF.	DEBIT	CREDIT	BALANCE DEBIT	BALANCE CREDIT

ACCOUNT *Accounts Receivable* ACCOUNT NO. *12*

DATE		ITEM	POST. REF.	DEBIT	CREDIT	BALANCE DEBIT	BALANCE CREDIT

ACCOUNT *Prepaid Insurance* ACCOUNT NO. *13*

DATE		ITEM	POST. REF.	DEBIT	CREDIT	BALANCE DEBIT	BALANCE CREDIT

PROBLEM 2-4 ___, Continued

ACCOUNT *Office Supplies* ACCOUNT NO. *14*

DATE		ITEM	POST. REF.	DEBIT	CREDIT	BALANCE	
						DEBIT	CREDIT

ACCOUNT *Land* ACCOUNT NO. *16*

DATE		ITEM	POST. REF.	DEBIT	CREDIT	BALANCE	
						DEBIT	CREDIT

ACCOUNT *Accounts Payable* ACCOUNT NO. *21*

DATE		ITEM	POST. REF.	DEBIT	CREDIT	BALANCE	
						DEBIT	CREDIT

ACCOUNT *Unearned Rent* ACCOUNT NO. *22*

DATE		ITEM	POST. REF.	DEBIT	CREDIT	BALANCE	
						DEBIT	CREDIT

ACCOUNT *Notes Payable* ACCOUNT NO. *23*

DATE		ITEM	POST. REF.	DEBIT	CREDIT	BALANCE	
						DEBIT	CREDIT

PROBLEM 2-4 ___, Continued

ACCOUNT ______________________, *Capital* ACCOUNT NO. *31*

DATE		ITEM	POST. REF.	DEBIT	CREDIT	BALANCE DEBIT	BALANCE CREDIT

ACCOUNT ______________________, *Drawing* ACCOUNT NO. *32*

DATE		ITEM	POST. REF.	DEBIT	CREDIT	BALANCE DEBIT	BALANCE CREDIT

ACCOUNT *Fees Earned* ACCOUNT NO. *41*

DATE		ITEM	POST. REF.	DEBIT	CREDIT	BALANCE DEBIT	BALANCE CREDIT

ACCOUNT *Salary and Commission Expense* ACCOUNT NO. *51*

DATE		ITEM	POST. REF.	DEBIT	CREDIT	BALANCE DEBIT	BALANCE CREDIT

ACCOUNT *Rent Expense* ACCOUNT NO. *52*

DATE		ITEM	POST. REF.	DEBIT	CREDIT	BALANCE DEBIT	BALANCE CREDIT

PROBLEM 2-4 ___, Continued

ACCOUNT *Advertising Expense* ACCOUNT NO. *53*

DATE		ITEM	POST. REF.	DEBIT	CREDIT	BALANCE	
						DEBIT	CREDIT

ACCOUNT *Automobile Expense* ACCOUNT NO. *54*

DATE		ITEM	POST. REF.	DEBIT	CREDIT	BALANCE	
						DEBIT	CREDIT

ACCOUNT *Miscellaneous Expense* ACCOUNT NO. *59*

DATE		ITEM	POST. REF.	DEBIT	CREDIT	BALANCE	
						DEBIT	CREDIT

PROBLEM 2-4 ___, Concluded

4.

Unadjusted Trial Balance

5. a. ______________________

b.

JOURNAL PAGE *19*

	DATE		DESCRIPTION	POST. REF.	DEBIT	CREDIT	
1							1
2							2
3							3
4							4

c. ______________________

This Page Not Used.

Name ______________________________

PROBLEM 2-5 ___

1.

Corrected Unadjusted Trial Balance

	DEBIT BALANCES	CREDIT BALANCES
Cash		
Accounts Receivable		
Supplies		
Prepaid Insurance		
Equipment		
Notes Payable		
Accounts Payable		
________________, *Capital*		
________________, *Drawing*		
Fees Earned		
Wages Expense		
Rent Expense		
Advertising Expense		
Gas, Electricity, and Water Expense		
Miscellaneous Expense		

2. ____

This Page Not Used.

Name ______________________________

CONTINUING PROBLEM

2. and 3.

JOURNAL

PAGE 1

	DATE		DESCRIPTION	POST. REF.	DEBIT	CREDIT	
1							1
2							2
3							3
4							4
5							5
6							6
7							7
8							8
9							9
10							10
11							11
12							12
13							13
14							14
15							15
16							16
17							17
18							18
19							19
20							20
21							21
22							22
23							23
24							24
25							25
26							26
27							27
28							28
29							29
30							30
31							31
32							32
33							33
34							34
35							35

CONTINUING PROBLEM, Continued

JOURNAL

PAGE 2

	DATE		DESCRIPTION	POST. REF.	DEBIT	CREDIT	
1							1
2							2
3							3
4							4
5							5
6							6
7							7
8							8
9							9
10							10
11							11
12							12
13							13
14							14
15							15
16							16
17							17
18							18
19							19
20							20
21							21
22							22
23							23
24							24
25							25
26							26
27							27
28							28
29							29
30							30
31							31
32							32
33							33
34							34
35							35
36							36

Name ______________________________

CONTINUING PROBLEM, Continued

JOURNAL

PAGE 2
continued

	DATE		DESCRIPTION	POST. REF.	DEBIT	CREDIT	
1							1
2							2
3							3
4							4
5							5
6							6
7							7
8							8
9							9
10							10
11							11
12							12
13							13
14							14
15							15
16							16
17							17
18							18
19							19
20							20
21							21
22							22
23							23
24							24
25							25
26							26
27							27
28							28
29							29
30							30
31							31
32							32
33							33
34							34
35							35

CONTINUING PROBLEM, Continued

1. and 3.

GENERAL LEDGER

ACCOUNT *Cash* ACCOUNT NO. *11*

DATE		ITEM	POST. REF.	DEBIT	CREDIT	BALANCE	
						DEBIT	CREDIT

Name ______________________________

CONTINUING PROBLEM, Continued

ACCOUNT *Accounts Receivable* ACCOUNT NO. *12*

DATE		ITEM	POST. REF.	DEBIT	CREDIT	BALANCE	
						DEBIT	CREDIT

ACCOUNT *Supplies* ACCOUNT NO. *14*

DATE		ITEM	POST. REF.	DEBIT	CREDIT	BALANCE	
						DEBIT	CREDIT

ACCOUNT *Prepaid Insurance* ACCOUNT NO. *15*

DATE		ITEM	POST. REF.	DEBIT	CREDIT	BALANCE	
						DEBIT	CREDIT

ACCOUNT *Office Equipment* ACCOUNT NO. *17*

DATE		ITEM	POST. REF.	DEBIT	CREDIT	BALANCE	
						DEBIT	CREDIT

CONTINUING PROBLEM, Continued

ACCOUNT *Accumulated Depreciation—Office Equipment* ACCOUNT NO. *18*

DATE		ITEM	POST. REF.	DEBIT	CREDIT	BALANCE	
						DEBIT	CREDIT

(This account is not used in Chapter 2.)

ACCOUNT *Accounts Payable* ACCOUNT NO. *21*

DATE		ITEM	POST. REF.	DEBIT	CREDIT	BALANCE	
						DEBIT	CREDIT

ACCOUNT *Wages Payable* ACCOUNT NO. *22*

DATE		ITEM	POST. REF.	DEBIT	CREDIT	BALANCE	
						DEBIT	CREDIT

(This account is not used in Chapter 2.)

ACCOUNT *Unearned Revenue* ACCOUNT NO. *23*

DATE		ITEM	POST. REF.	DEBIT	CREDIT	BALANCE	
						DEBIT	CREDIT

Name ______________________________

CONTINUING PROBLEM, Continued

ACCOUNT *Peyton Smith, Capital* ACCOUNT NO. *31*

DATE		ITEM	POST. REF.	DEBIT	CREDIT	BALANCE	
						DEBIT	CREDIT

ACCOUNT *Peyton Smith, Drawing* ACCOUNT NO. *32*

DATE		ITEM	POST. REF.	DEBIT	CREDIT	BALANCE	
						DEBIT	CREDIT

ACCOUNT *Fees Earned* ACCOUNT NO. *41*

DATE		ITEM	POST. REF.	DEBIT	CREDIT	BALANCE	
						DEBIT	CREDIT

CONTINUING PROBLEM, Continued

ACCOUNT *Wages Expense* ACCOUNT NO. *50*

DATE		ITEM	POST. REF.	DEBIT	CREDIT	BALANCE DEBIT	BALANCE CREDIT

ACCOUNT *Office Rent Expense* ACCOUNT NO. *51*

DATE		ITEM	POST. REF.	DEBIT	CREDIT	BALANCE DEBIT	BALANCE CREDIT

ACCOUNT *Equipment Rent Expense* ACCOUNT NO. *52*

DATE		ITEM	POST. REF.	DEBIT	CREDIT	BALANCE DEBIT	BALANCE CREDIT

ACCOUNT *Utilities Expense* ACCOUNT NO. *53*

DATE		ITEM	POST. REF.	DEBIT	CREDIT	BALANCE DEBIT	BALANCE CREDIT

Name ______________________________

CONTINUING PROBLEM, Continued

ACCOUNT *Music Expense* ACCOUNT NO. *54*

DATE		ITEM	POST. REF.	DEBIT	CREDIT	BALANCE DEBIT	BALANCE CREDIT

ACCOUNT *Advertising Expense* ACCOUNT NO. *55*

DATE		ITEM	POST. REF.	DEBIT	CREDIT	BALANCE DEBIT	BALANCE CREDIT

ACCOUNT *Supplies Expense* ACCOUNT NO. *56*

DATE		ITEM	POST. REF.	DEBIT	CREDIT	BALANCE DEBIT	BALANCE CREDIT

ACCOUNT *Insurance Expense* ACCOUNT NO. *57*

DATE		ITEM	POST. REF.	DEBIT	CREDIT	BALANCE DEBIT	BALANCE CREDIT

(This account is not used in Chapter 2.)

CONTINUING PROBLEM, Continued

ACCOUNT *Depreciation Expense* ACCOUNT NO. *58*

DATE		ITEM	POST. REF.	DEBIT	CREDIT	BALANCE DEBIT	BALANCE CREDIT

(This account is not used in Chapter 2.)

ACCOUNT *Miscellaneous Expense* ACCOUNT NO. *59*

DATE		ITEM	POST. REF.	DEBIT	CREDIT	BALANCE DEBIT	BALANCE CREDIT

CONTINUING PROBLEM, Concluded

4.

Unadjusted Trial Balance

This Page Not Used.

Name ______________________________

EXERCISE 3-1

1. Bills for ads that appeared in prior month's local newspaper: ______________________
2. Fees received but not yet earned: ______________________
3. Fees earned but not yet received: ______________________
4. Premium paid on a one-year insurance policy: ______________________
5. Rent received in advance for rental of office space: ______________________
6. Supplies on hand: ______________________
7. Rent paid in advance: ______________________
8. Wages owed but payable in the following period: ______________________

EXERCISE 3-2

Account	Answer
Accounts Receivable	Normally requires adjustment (AR).
Cash..	
Harriet Kasun, Capital...............	
Interest Expense.......................	
Interest Receivable..................	
Land..	
Office Equipment	
Prepaid Rent............................	
Supplies	
Unearned Fees.........................	
Wages Expense.......................	

EXERCISE 3-3

a.

JOURNAL PAGE

	DATE		DESCRIPTION	POST. REF.	DEBIT	CREDIT	
1							1
2							2
3							3
4							4

b. ______________________

EXERCISE 3-4

a. ______________________

b. ______________________

EXERCISE 3-5

a. and b.

JOURNAL PAGE

	DATE		DESCRIPTION	POST. REF.	DEBIT	CREDIT	
1							1
2							2
3							3
4							4
5							5
6							6
7							7
8							8
9							9
10							10

EXERCISE 3-6

EXERCISE 3-7

a.

b.

EXERCISE 3-8

a.

b.

EXERCISE 3-9

JOURNAL PAGE

	DATE		DESCRIPTION	POST. REF.	DEBIT	CREDIT	
1							1
2							2
3							3
4							4

EXERCISE 3-10

a.

b.

EXERCISE 3-11

JOURNAL PAGE

	DATE		DESCRIPTION	POST. REF.	DEBIT	CREDIT	
1							1
2							2
3							3
4							4

EXERCISE 3-12

____

EXERCISE 3-13

a. ______________________________

____

____

b. ______________________________

____

____

EXERCISE 3-14

a. and b.

JOURNAL PAGE

	DATE		DESCRIPTION	POST. REF.	DEBIT	CREDIT	
1							1
2							2
3							3
4							4
5							5
6							6
7							7
8							8

Name ______________________

EXERCISE 3-15

a. and b.

JOURNAL PAGE

	DATE		DESCRIPTION	POST. REF.	DEBIT	CREDIT	
1							1
2							2
3							3
4							4
5							5
6							6
7							7
8							8

EXERCISE 3-16

a. and b.

JOURNAL PAGE

	DATE		DESCRIPTION	POST. REF.	DEBIT	CREDIT	
1							1
2							2
3							3
4							4
5							5
6							6
7							7
8							8

EXERCISE 3-17

a.

JOURNAL PAGE

	DATE		DESCRIPTION	POST. REF.	DEBIT	CREDIT	
1							1
2							2
3							3
4							4
5							5
6							6
7							7
8							8
9							9
10							10

b. ____

EXERCISE 3-18

JOURNAL PAGE

	DATE		DESCRIPTION	POST. REF.	DEBIT	CREDIT	
1							1
2							2
3							3
4							4

EXERCISE 3-19

a. ____

b. ____

____

____

____

Name ________________________________

EXERCISE 3-20

a. ____

b. ____

____

____

____

____

EXERCISE 3-21

____

EXERCISE 3-22

a. ____

b. ____

EXERCISE 3-23

	Error (a)		Error (b)	
	Overstated	Understated	Overstated	Understated
1. Revenue for the year would be	$	$	$	$
2. Expenses for the year would be	$	$	$	$
3. Net income for the year would be	$	$	$	$
4. Assets at July 31 would be	$	$	$	$
5. Liabilities at July 31 would be	$	$	$	$
6. Owner's equity at July 31 would be	$	$	$	$

EXERCISE 3-24

____

____

EXERCISE 3-25

a.

JOURNAL PAGE

	DATE		DESCRIPTION	POST. REF.	DEBIT	CREDIT	
1							1
2							2
3							3
4							4

b. (1) ____________________

(2) ____________________

Name ______________________________

EXERCISE 3-26

JOURNAL

PAGE

	DATE		DESCRIPTION	POST. REF.	DEBIT	CREDIT	
1							1
2							2
3							3
4							4
5							5
6							6
7							7
8							8
9							9
10							10
11							11
12							12
13							13
14							14
15							15
16							16
17							17
18							18
19							19
20							20
21							21
22							22

EXERCISE 3-27

Name ____________________________

EXERCISE 3-27, Concluded

(Optional)

Adjusted Trial Balance

EXERCISE 3-28

a.

Operating Income Statements

(in millions)

	YEAR 2		YEAR 1	
	AMOUNT	PERCENT	AMOUNT	PERCENT

b.

Name ________________________

EXERCISE 3-29

a. ________________________

____

____

____

b. ________________________

____

____

____

____

c. ________________________

____

____

____

____

____

EXERCISE 3-30

a.

	AMOUNT	PERCENT

b.

	AMOUNT	PERCENT

c.

Name ____________________________________

PROBLEM 3-1 ___

1.

JOURNAL

PAGE

	DATE		DESCRIPTION	POST. REF.	DEBIT	CREDIT	
1							1
2							2
3							3
4							4
5							5
6							6
7							7
8							8
9							9
10							10
11							11
12							12
13							13
14							14
15							15
16							16
17							17
18							18
19							19
20							20
21							21
22							22
23							23
24							24

2. ____

This Page Not Used.

Name ______________________________

PROBLEM 3-2 ___

1.

JOURNAL

PAGE

	DATE		DESCRIPTION	POST. REF.	DEBIT	CREDIT	
1							1
2							2
3							3
4							4
5							5
6							6
7							7
8							8
9							9
10							10
11							11
12							12
13							13
14							14
15							15
16							16
17							17
18							18
19							19
20							20
21							21
22							22
23							23
24							24
25							25
26							26
27							27
28							28
29							29
30							30
31							31
32							32
33							33
34							34
35							35

PROBLEM 3-2 ___, Concluded

2. ____

____

____

____

3. ____

____

____

____

____

____

____

____

____

____

4. ____

____

____

____

Name ____________________________________

PROBLEM 3-3 ___

1.

JOURNAL

PAGE

	DATE		DESCRIPTION	POST. REF.	DEBIT	CREDIT	
1							1
2							2
3							3
4							4
5							5
6							6
7							7
8							8
9							9
10							10
11							11
12							12
13							13
14							14
15							15
16							16
17							17
18							18
19							19
20							20
21							21
22							22
23							23
24							24
25							25
26							26
27							27
28							28
29							29
30							30
31							31
32							32
33							33
34							34
35							35

PROBLEM 3-3 ___, Concluded

2.

	AMOUNT

3.

	AMOUNT

4. ______________________________

Name ______________________________

PROBLEM 3-4 ___

JOURNAL

PAGE

DATE		DESCRIPTION	POST. REF.	DEBIT	CREDIT

PROBLEM 3-4 ___, Concluded

JOURNAL

PAGE

	DATE		DESCRIPTION	POST. REF.	DEBIT	CREDIT	
1							1
2							2
3							3
4							4
5							5
6							6
7							7
8							8
9							9
10							10
11							11
12							12
13							13
14							14
15							15
16							16
17							17
18							18
19							19
20							20
21							21
22							22
23							23
24							24
25							25
26							26
27							27
28							28
29							29
30							30
31							31
32							32
33							33
34							34
35							35
36							36

Name ______________________________

PROBLEM 3-5 ___

1.

JOURNAL

PAGE

DATE		DESCRIPTION	POST. REF.	DEBIT	CREDIT

PROBLEM 3-5 ___, Concluded

2.

Adjusted Trial Balance

Name ______________________________

PROBLEM 3-6 ___

1.

JOURNAL PAGE

DATE		DESCRIPTION	POST. REF.	DEBIT	CREDIT	
1						1
2						2
3						3
4						4
5						5
6						6
7						7
8						8
9						9
10						10
11						11
12						12
13						13
14						14
15						15
16						16
17						17
18						18
19						19
20						20

2.

	Net Income	Total Assets	=	Total Liabilities	+	Total Owner's Equity
Reported amounts	$	$		$		$
Corrections:						
Adjustment (a)						
Adjustment (b)						
Adjustment (c)						
Adjustment (d)						
Corrected amounts	$	$		$		$

This Page Not Used.

Name ______________________________

CONTINUING PROBLEM

1.

JOURNAL

PAGE 3

DATE		DESCRIPTION	POST. REF.	DEBIT	CREDIT

CONTINUING PROBLEM, Continued

2.

GENERAL LEDGER

ACCOUNT *Cash* ACCOUNT NO. *11*

DATE		ITEM	POST. REF.	DEBIT	CREDIT	BALANCE	
						DEBIT	CREDIT

Name ______________________________

CONTINUING PROBLEM, Continued

ACCOUNT *Accounts Receivable* ACCOUNT NO. *12*

DATE		ITEM	POST. REF.	DEBIT	CREDIT	BALANCE	
						DEBIT	CREDIT

ACCOUNT *Supplies* ACCOUNT NO. *14*

DATE		ITEM	POST. REF.	DEBIT	CREDIT	BALANCE	
						DEBIT	CREDIT

ACCOUNT *Prepaid Insurance* ACCOUNT NO. *15*

DATE		ITEM	POST. REF.	DEBIT	CREDIT	BALANCE	
						DEBIT	CREDIT

ACCOUNT *Office Equipment* ACCOUNT NO. *17*

DATE		ITEM	POST. REF.	DEBIT	CREDIT	BALANCE	
						DEBIT	CREDIT

CONTINUING PROBLEM, Continued

ACCOUNT *Accumulated Depreciation—Office Equipment* ACCOUNT NO. *18*

DATE		ITEM	POST. REF.	DEBIT	CREDIT	BALANCE	
						DEBIT	CREDIT

ACCOUNT *Accounts Payable* ACCOUNT NO. *21*

DATE		ITEM	POST. REF.	DEBIT	CREDIT	BALANCE	
						DEBIT	CREDIT

ACCOUNT *Wages Payable* ACCOUNT NO. *22*

DATE		ITEM	POST. REF.	DEBIT	CREDIT	BALANCE	
						DEBIT	CREDIT

ACCOUNT *Unearned Revenue* ACCOUNT NO. *23*

DATE		ITEM	POST. REF.	DEBIT	CREDIT	BALANCE	
						DEBIT	CREDIT

Name ___________________________

CONTINUING PROBLEM, Continued

ACCOUNT *Peyton Smith, Capital* ACCOUNT NO. *31*

DATE		ITEM	POST. REF.	DEBIT	CREDIT	BALANCE	
						DEBIT	CREDIT

ACCOUNT *Peyton Smith, Drawing* ACCOUNT NO. *32*

DATE		ITEM	POST. REF.	DEBIT	CREDIT	BALANCE	
						DEBIT	CREDIT

ACCOUNT *Fees Earned* ACCOUNT NO. *41*

DATE		ITEM	POST. REF.	DEBIT	CREDIT	BALANCE	
						DEBIT	CREDIT

CONTINUING PROBLEM, Continued

ACCOUNT *Wages Expense* ACCOUNT NO. *50*

DATE		ITEM	POST. REF.	DEBIT	CREDIT	BALANCE DEBIT	BALANCE CREDIT

ACCOUNT *Office Rent Expense* ACCOUNT NO. *51*

DATE		ITEM	POST. REF.	DEBIT	CREDIT	BALANCE DEBIT	BALANCE CREDIT

ACCOUNT *Equipment Rent Expense* ACCOUNT NO. *52*

DATE		ITEM	POST. REF.	DEBIT	CREDIT	BALANCE DEBIT	BALANCE CREDIT

ACCOUNT *Utilities Expense* ACCOUNT NO. *53*

DATE		ITEM	POST. REF.	DEBIT	CREDIT	BALANCE DEBIT	BALANCE CREDIT

Name ______________________________

CONTINUING PROBLEM, Continued

ACCOUNT *Music Expense* ACCOUNT NO. *54*

DATE	ITEM	POST. REF.	DEBIT	CREDIT	BALANCE	
					DEBIT	CREDIT

ACCOUNT *Advertising Expense* ACCOUNT NO. *55*

DATE	ITEM	POST. REF.	DEBIT	CREDIT	BALANCE	
					DEBIT	CREDIT

ACCOUNT *Supplies Expense* ACCOUNT NO. *56*

DATE	ITEM	POST. REF.	DEBIT	CREDIT	BALANCE	
					DEBIT	CREDIT

ACCOUNT *Insurance Expense* ACCOUNT NO. *57*

DATE	ITEM	POST. REF.	DEBIT	CREDIT	BALANCE	
					DEBIT	CREDIT

CONTINUING PROBLEM, Continued

ACCOUNT *Depreciation Expense* ACCOUNT NO. *58*

DATE		ITEM	POST. REF.	DEBIT	CREDIT	BALANCE	
						DEBIT	CREDIT

ACCOUNT *Miscellaneous Expense* ACCOUNT NO. *59*

DATE		ITEM	POST. REF.	DEBIT	CREDIT	BALANCE	
						DEBIT	CREDIT

Name ________________________________

CONTINUING PROBLEM, Concluded

3.

Adjusted Trial Balance			

This Page Not Used.

Name ______________________________

EXERCISE 4-1

1. Accounts Payable: ______________________________
2. Accounts Receivable: ______________________________
3. Cash: ______________________________
4. Eddy Rosewood, Drawing: ______________________________
5. Fees Earned: ______________________________
6. Supplies: ______________________________
7. Unearned Rent: ______________________________
8. Utilities Expense: ______________________________
9. Wages Expense: ______________________________
10. Wages Payable: ______________________________

EXERCISE 4-2

1. Accounts Receivable: ______________________________
2. Equipment: ______________________________
3. Fees Earned: ______________________________
4. Insurance Expense: ______________________________
5. Land: ______________________________
6. Prepaid Rent: ______________________________
7. Rent Revenue: ______________________________
8. Salary Expense: ______________________________
9. Salary Payable: ______________________________
10. Supplies: ______________________________
11. Unearned Rent: ______________________________
12. Wages Payable: ______________________________

EXERCISE 4-3

Income Statement

Statement of Owner's Equity

Name ______________________________

EXERCISE 4-3, Concluded

Balance Sheet

EXERCISE 4-4

Income Statement

Statement of Owner's Equity

Name ______________________________

EXERCISE 4-4, Concluded

Balance Sheet

EXERCISE 4-5

Income Statement

EXERCISE 4-6

Income Statement

Name ______________________________

EXERCISE 4-7

Income Statement

(in millions)

EXERCISE 4-8

Statement of Owner's Equity

EXERCISE 4-9

Statement of Owner's Equity

EXERCISE 4-10

1. Accounts Receivable: ______________________________
2. Building: ______________________________
3. Cash: ______________________________
4. Land: ______________________________
5. Prepaid Insurance: ______________________________
6. Supplies: ______________________________

EXERCISE 4-11

____

____

____

____

____

____

____

Name ______________________________

EXERCISE 4-12

Balance Sheet

EXERCISE 4-13

EXERCISE 4-13, Concluded

Balance Sheet

EXERCISE 4-14

a. Accounts Receivable: ______________________

b. Accumulated Depreciation: ______________________

c. Building: ______________________

d. Depreciation Expense: ______________________

e. Fees Earned: ______________________

f. Jackie Lindsay, Capital: ______________________

g. Jackie Lindsay, Drawing: ______________________

h. Land: ______________________

i. Supplies: ______________________

j. Supplies Expense: ______________________

k. Unearned Rent: ______________________

l. Wages Expense: ______________________

EXERCISE 4-15

____

____

EXERCISE 4-16

a.

JOURNAL PAGE

	DATE		DESCRIPTION	POST. REF.	DEBIT	CREDIT	
1							1
2							2
3							3
4							4

b. ______________________

____

Name ____________________

EXERCISE 4-17

JOURNAL

PAGE

	DATE		DESCRIPTION	POST. REF.	DEBIT	CREDIT	
1							1
2							2
3							3
4							4
5							5
6							6
7							7
8							8
9							9
10							10
11							11
12							12
13							13
14							14

EXERCISE 4-18

a. Accounts Receivable: ____________________

b. Cash: ____________________

c. Depreciation Expense: ____________________

d. Fees Earned: ____________________

e. Doug Woods, Capital: ____________________

f. Doug Woods, Drawing: ____________________

g. Equipment: ____________________

h. Land: ____________________

i. Salaries Payable: ____________________

j. Unearned Rent: ____________________

k. Wages Expense: ____________________

EXERCISE 4-19

Post-Closing Trial Balance

EXERCISE 4-20

a. ____________________
b. ____________________
c. ____________________
d. ____________________
e. ____________________
f. ____________________
g. ____________________
h. ____________________
i. ____________________
j. ____________________

Name ______________________

EXERCISE 4-21

a.

	December 31	
	Year 2	**Year 1**
Current assets	$1,498,763	$1,549,399
Current liabilities	478,810	421,627
Working capital	________	________
Current ratio	________	________

b. ____

____

____

____

____

____

____

EXERCISE 4-22

a.

	Year 2	**Year 1**
Current assets	$4,352,700	$4,168,700
Current liabilities	3,653,500	3,038,700
Working capital	________	________
Current ratio	________	________

b. ____

____

____

____

____

____

____

____

APPENDIX 1 EXERCISE 4-23

1. ____________________
2. ____________________
3. ____________________
4. ____________________
5. ____________________
6. ____________________
7. ____________________
8. ____________________
9. ____________________
10. ____________________

Name ____________________

APPENDIX 1 EXERCISE 4-24

	A	B	C	D	E	F	G	H	I	J	K
1	ALERT SECURITY SERVICES CO.										
2	End-of-Period Spreadsheet (Work Sheet)										
3	For the Year Ended October 31, 2019										
4–5		Unadjusted Trial Balance		Adjustments		Adjusted Trial Balance		Income Statement		Balance Sheet	
6	Account Title	Dr.	Cr.	Dr.	Cr.	Dr.	Cr.	Dr.	Cr.	Dr.	Cr.
7	Cash	12									
8	Accounts Receivable	90									
9	Supplies	8									
10	Prepaid Insurance	12									
11	Land	190									
12	Equipment	50									
13	Accum. Depr.—Equipment		4								
14	Accounts Payable		36								
15	Wages Payable		0								
16	Brenda Schultz, Capital		260								
17	Brenda Schultz, Drawing	8									
18	Fees Earned		200								
19	Wages Expense	110									
20	Rent Expense	12									
21	Insurance Expense	0									
22	Utilities Expense	6									
23	Supplies Expense	0									
24	Depreciation Expense	0									
25	Miscellaneous Expense	2									
26	Totals	500	500								
27											
28											
29											
30											
31											

APPENDIX 1 EXERCISE 4-25

ALERT SECURITY SERVICES CO.
End-of-Period Spreadsheet (Work Sheet)
For the Year Ended October 31, 2019

	A	B	C	D	E	F	G	H	I	J	K
4–5		Unadjusted Trial Balance		Adjustments		Adjusted Trial Balance		Income Statement		Balance Sheet	
6	**Account Title**	Dr.	Cr.	Dr.	Cr.	Dr.	Cr.	Dr.	Cr.	Dr.	Cr.
7	Cash					12					
8	Accounts Receivable					103					
9	Supplies					4					
10	Prepaid Insurance					2					
11	Land					190					
12	Equipment					50					
13	Accum. Depr.—Equipment						7				
14	Accounts Payable						36				
15	Wages Payable						1				
16	Brenda Schultz, Capital						260				
17	Brenda Schultz, Drawing					8					
18	Fees Earned						213				
19	Wages Expense					111					
20	Rent Expense					12					
21	Insurance Expense					10					
22	Utilities Expense					6					
23	Supplies Expense					4					
24	Depreciation Expense					3					
25	Miscellaneous Expense					2					
26	Totals					517	517				
27	Net income (loss)										
28											
29											
30											
31											

APPENDIX 1 EXERCISE 4-26

Income Statement

Statement of Owner's Equity

Name ______________________

APPENDIX 1 EXERCISE 4-26, Concluded

Balance Sheet

APPENDIX 1 EXERCISE 4-27

JOURNAL

PAGE

	DATE		DESCRIPTION	POST. REF.	DEBIT	CREDIT	
1							1
2							2
3							3
4							4
5							5
6							6
7							7
8							8
9							9
10							10
11							11
12							12
13							13
14							14
15							15
16							16
17							17
18							18
19							19
20							20
21							21
22							22
23							23
24							24

Name ______________________________

APPENDIX 1 EXERCISE 4-28

JOURNAL

PAGE ______

	DATE		DESCRIPTION	POST. REF.	DEBIT	CREDIT	
1							1
2							2
3							3
4							4
5							5
6							6
7							7
8							8
9							9
10							10
11							11
12							12
13							13
14							14
15							15
16							16
17							17
18							18
19							19
20							20

APPENDIX 2 EXERCISE 4-29

a., b., and c.

JOURNAL PAGE

	DATE		DESCRIPTION	POST. REF.	DEBIT	CREDIT	
1							1
2							2
3							3
4							4
5							5
6							6
7							7
8							8
9							9
10							10

d. ____________________

Name ______________________________

APPENDIX 2 EXERCISE 4-30

a. and b.

JOURNAL

PAGE

	DATE		DESCRIPTION	POST. REF.	DEBIT	CREDIT	
1							1
2							2
3							3
4							4
5							5
6							6
7							7
8							8
9							9
10							10
11							11
12							12
13							13
14							14
15							15
16							16
17							17
18							18
19							19
20							20

APPENDIX 2 EXERCISE 4-31

a. and b.

JOURNAL

PAGE

	DATE		DESCRIPTION	POST. REF.	DEBIT	CREDIT	
1							1
2							2
3							3
4							4
5							5
6							6
7							7
8							8
9							9
10							10
11							11
12							12
13							13
14							14
15							15
16							16
17							17
18							18
19							19
20							20

Name ______________________________

APPENDIX 2 EXERCISE 4-32

a. (1) ______________________________

(2) ______________________________

(3) ______________________________

(4) ______________________________

(5) ______________________________

b.

JOURNAL

PAGE

	DATE		DESCRIPTION	POST. REF.	DEBIT	CREDIT	
1							1
2							2
3							3
4							4
5							5
6							6
7							7
8							8
9							9
10							10
11							11
12							12
13							13
14							14
15							15
16							16
17							17
18							18
19							19
20							20

APPENDIX 2 EXERCISE 4-33

a. (1) ______________________

(2) ______________________

(3) ______________________

(4) ______________________

(5) ______________________

b.

JOURNAL

PAGE

	DATE		DESCRIPTION	POST. REF.	DEBIT	CREDIT	
1							1
2							2
3							3
4							4
5							5
6							6
7							7
8							8
9							9
10							10
11							11
12							12
13							13
14							14
15							15
16							16
17							17
18							18
19							19
20							20

PROBLEM 4-1 ___

1.

Income Statement

2.

Statement of Owner's Equity

PROBLEM 4-1 ___, Continued

3.

Balance Sheet

Name ______________________________

PROBLEM 4-1 ___, Continued

4.

JOURNAL PAGE

DATE		DESCRIPTION	POST. REF.	DEBIT	CREDIT
		Closing Entries			

PROBLEM 4-1 ___, Concluded

5.

Post-Closing Trial Balance

Name ______________________________

PROBLEM 4-2 ___

1.

Income Statement

Statement of Owner's Equity

PROBLEM 4-2 ___, Continued

Balance Sheet

Name ______________________

PROBLEM 4-2 ___, Concluded

2.

JOURNAL PAGE

	DATE		DESCRIPTION	POST. REF.	DEBIT	CREDIT	
1			*Closing Entries*				1
2							2
3							3
4							4
5							5
6							6
7							7
8							8
9							9
10							10
11							11
12							12
13							13
14							14
15							15
16							16
17							17
18							18
19							19
20							20
21							21
22							22
23							23
24							24

3. ______________________

This Page Not Used.

Name ______________________________

PROBLEM 4-3 ___

1., 3., and 6.

Cash

Laundry Supplies

Prepaid Insurance

Laundry Equipment

Accumulated Depreciation

Accounts Payable

PROBLEM 4-3 ___, Continued

Wages Payable

____________________, Capital

____________________, Drawing

Laundry Revenue

Wages Expense

Rent Expense

Name ____________________

PROBLEM 4-3 ___, Continued

Utilities Expense

Laundry Supplies Expense

Depreciation Expense

Insurance Expense

Miscellaneous Expense

Name ______________________

PROBLEM 4-3 ___, Continued

2. Optional (Appendix)

	A	B	C	D	E	F	G	H	I	J	K
2	End-of-Period Spreadsheet (Work Sheet)										
3											
4		Unadjusted Trial Balance		Adjustments		Adjusted Trial Balance		Income Statement		Balance Sheet	
5											
6	Account Title	Dr.	Cr.	Dr.	Cr.	Dr.	Cr.	Dr.	Cr.	Dr.	Cr.
7											
8											
9											
10											
12											
13											
14											
15											
16											
17											
18											
19											
20											
22											
23											
24											
25											
26											
27											
28											
29											
30											

Name ______________________

PROBLEM 4-3 ___, Continued

3.

JOURNAL

PAGE

DATE		DESCRIPTION	POST. REF.	DEBIT	CREDIT
		Adjusting Entries			

PROBLEM 4-3 ___, Continued

4.

Adjusted Trial Balance

Name ______________________________

PROBLEM 4-3 ___, Continued

5.

Income Statement

Statement of Owner's Equity

PROBLEM 4-3 ___, Continued

Balance Sheet

PROBLEM 4-3 ___, Continued

6.

JOURNAL

PAGE

DATE		DESCRIPTION	POST. REF.	DEBIT	CREDIT
		Closing Entries			

PROBLEM 4-3 ___, Concluded

7.

Post-Closing Trial Balance

Name ______________________________

PROBLEM 4-4 ___

1., 3., and 6.

GENERAL LEDGER

ACCOUNT *Cash* ACCOUNT NO. *11*

DATE	ITEM	POST. REF.	DEBIT	CREDIT	BALANCE	
					DEBIT	CREDIT

ACCOUNT *Supplies* ACCOUNT NO. *13*

DATE	ITEM	POST. REF.	DEBIT	CREDIT	BALANCE	
					DEBIT	CREDIT

ACCOUNT *Prepaid Insurance* ACCOUNT NO. *14*

DATE	ITEM	POST. REF.	DEBIT	CREDIT	BALANCE	
					DEBIT	CREDIT

ACCOUNT *Equipment* ACCOUNT NO. *16*

DATE	ITEM	POST. REF.	DEBIT	CREDIT	BALANCE	
					DEBIT	CREDIT

ACCOUNT *Accumulated Depreciation—Equipment* ACCOUNT NO. *17*

DATE	ITEM	POST. REF.	DEBIT	CREDIT	BALANCE	
					DEBIT	CREDIT

PROBLEM 4-4 ___, Continued

ACCOUNT *Trucks* ACCOUNT NO. *18*

DATE		ITEM	POST. REF.	DEBIT	CREDIT	BALANCE DEBIT	BALANCE CREDIT

ACCOUNT *Accumulated Depreciation—Trucks* ACCOUNT NO. *19*

DATE		ITEM	POST. REF.	DEBIT	CREDIT	BALANCE DEBIT	BALANCE CREDIT

ACCOUNT *Accounts Payable* ACCOUNT NO. *21*

DATE		ITEM	POST. REF.	DEBIT	CREDIT	BALANCE DEBIT	BALANCE CREDIT

ACCOUNT *Wages Payable* ACCOUNT NO. *22*

DATE		ITEM	POST. REF.	DEBIT	CREDIT	BALANCE DEBIT	BALANCE CREDIT

ACCOUNT ______________________, *Capital* ACCOUNT NO. *31*

DATE		ITEM	POST. REF.	DEBIT	CREDIT	BALANCE DEBIT	BALANCE CREDIT

Name ______________________________

PROBLEM 4-4 ___, Continued

ACCOUNT ____________________, *Drawing* ACCOUNT NO. 32

DATE		ITEM	POST. REF.	DEBIT	CREDIT	BALANCE DEBIT	BALANCE CREDIT

ACCOUNT *Service Revenue* ACCOUNT NO. 41

DATE		ITEM	POST. REF.	DEBIT	CREDIT	BALANCE DEBIT	BALANCE CREDIT

ACCOUNT *Wages Expense* ACCOUNT NO. 51

DATE		ITEM	POST. REF.	DEBIT	CREDIT	BALANCE DEBIT	BALANCE CREDIT

ACCOUNT *Supplies Expense* ACCOUNT NO.

DATE		ITEM	POST. REF.	DEBIT	CREDIT	BALANCE DEBIT	BALANCE CREDIT

ACCOUNT *Rent Expense* ACCOUNT NO.

DATE		ITEM	POST. REF.	DEBIT	CREDIT	BALANCE DEBIT	BALANCE CREDIT

PROBLEM 4-4 ___, Continued

ACCOUNT *Truck Expense* ACCOUNT NO.

DATE		ITEM	POST. REF.	DEBIT	CREDIT	BALANCE DEBIT	BALANCE CREDIT

ACCOUNT *Depreciation Expense—Equipment* ACCOUNT NO.

DATE		ITEM	POST. REF.	DEBIT	CREDIT	BALANCE DEBIT	BALANCE CREDIT

ACCOUNT *Depreciation Expense—Trucks* ACCOUNT NO. *56*

DATE		ITEM	POST. REF.	DEBIT	CREDIT	BALANCE DEBIT	BALANCE CREDIT

ACCOUNT *Insurance Expense* ACCOUNT NO. *57*

DATE		ITEM	POST. REF.	DEBIT	CREDIT	BALANCE DEBIT	BALANCE CREDIT

ACCOUNT *Miscellaneous Expense* ACCOUNT NO. *59*

DATE		ITEM	POST. REF.	DEBIT	CREDIT	BALANCE DEBIT	BALANCE CREDIT

PROBLEM 4-4 ___, Continued

2. Optional (Appendix)

	A	B	C	D	E	F	G	H	I	J	K
1											
2	End-of-Period Spreadsheet (Work Sheet)										
3											
4		Unadjusted Trial Balance		Adjustments		Adjusted Trial Balance		Income Statement		Balance Sheet	
5											
6	Account Title	Dr.	Cr.	Dr.	Cr.	Dr.	Cr.	Dr.	Cr.	Dr.	Cr.
7											
8											
9											
10											
11											
12											
13											
14											
15											
16											
17											
18											
19											
20											
21											
22											
23											
24											
25											
26											
27											
28											
29											
30											

PROBLEM 4-4 ___, Continued

3.

JOURNAL

PAGE 26

DATE		DESCRIPTION	POST. REF.	DEBIT	CREDIT
		Adjusting Entries			

PROBLEM 4-4 ___, Continued

4.

Adjusted Trial Balance

PROBLEM 4-4 ___, Continued

5.

Income Statement

Statement of Owner's Equity

Name ______________________________

PROBLEM 4-4 ___, Continued

Balance Sheet

PROBLEM 4-4 ___, Continued

6.

JOURNAL

PAGE 27

DATE		DESCRIPTION	POST. REF.	DEBIT	CREDIT
		Closing Entries			

Name ________________________________

PROBLEM 4-4 ___, Concluded

7.

____

Post-Closing Trial Balance

____

This Page Not Used.

Name ______________________________

PROBLEM 4-5 ___

1. and 2.

JOURNAL

PAGE 1

	DATE		DESCRIPTION	POST. REF.	DEBIT	CREDIT	
1							1
2							2
3							3
4							4
5							5
6							6
7							7
8							8
9							9
10							10
11							11
12							12
13							13
14							14
15							15
16							16
17							17
18							18
19							19
20							20
21							21
22							22
23							23
24							24
25							25
26							26
27							27
28							28
29							29
30							30
31							31
32							32
33							33
34							34
35							35

PROBLEM 4-5 ___, Continued

JOURNAL

PAGE 2

	DATE		DESCRIPTION	POST. REF.	DEBIT	CREDIT	
1							1
2							2
3							3
4							4
5							5
6							6
7							7
8							8
9							9
10							10
11							11
12							12
13							13
14							14
15							15
16							16
17							17
18							18
19							19
20							20
21							21
22							22
23							23
24							24
25							25
26							26
27							27
28							28
29							29
30							30
31							31
32							32
33							33
34							34
35							35
36							36

PROBLEM 4-5 ___, Continued

2., 6., and 9.

GENERAL LEDGER

ACCOUNT *Cash* ACCOUNT NO. *11*

DATE		ITEM	POST. REF.	DEBIT	CREDIT	BALANCE	
						DEBIT	CREDIT

ACCOUNT *Accounts Receivable* ACCOUNT NO. *12*

DATE		ITEM	POST. REF.	DEBIT	CREDIT	BALANCE	
						DEBIT	CREDIT

PROBLEM 4-5 ___, Continued

ACCOUNT *Supplies* ACCOUNT NO. *14*

DATE		ITEM	POST. REF.	DEBIT	CREDIT	BALANCE DEBIT	BALANCE CREDIT

ACCOUNT *Prepaid Rent* ACCOUNT NO. *15*

DATE		ITEM	POST. REF.	DEBIT	CREDIT	BALANCE DEBIT	BALANCE CREDIT

ACCOUNT *Prepaid Insurance* ACCOUNT NO. *16*

DATE		ITEM	POST. REF.	DEBIT	CREDIT	BALANCE DEBIT	BALANCE CREDIT

ACCOUNT *Office Equipment* ACCOUNT NO. *18*

DATE		ITEM	POST. REF.	DEBIT	CREDIT	BALANCE DEBIT	BALANCE CREDIT

ACCOUNT *Accumulated Depreciation—Office Equipment* ACCOUNT NO. *19*

DATE		ITEM	POST. REF.	DEBIT	CREDIT	BALANCE DEBIT	BALANCE CREDIT

Name ______________________________

PROBLEM 4-5 ___, Continued

ACCOUNT *Accounts Payable* ACCOUNT NO. *21*

DATE		ITEM	POST. REF.	DEBIT	CREDIT	BALANCE	
						DEBIT	CREDIT

ACCOUNT *Salaries Payable* ACCOUNT NO. *22*

DATE		ITEM	POST. REF.	DEBIT	CREDIT	BALANCE	
						DEBIT	CREDIT

ACCOUNT *Unearned Fees* ACCOUNT NO. *23*

DATE		ITEM	POST. REF.	DEBIT	CREDIT	BALANCE	
						DEBIT	CREDIT

ACCOUNT ____________________, *Capital* ACCOUNT NO. *31*

DATE		ITEM	POST. REF.	DEBIT	CREDIT	BALANCE	
						DEBIT	CREDIT

ACCOUNT ____________________, *Drawing* ACCOUNT NO. *32*

DATE		ITEM	POST. REF.	DEBIT	CREDIT	BALANCE	
						DEBIT	CREDIT

PROBLEM 4-5 ___, Continued

ACCOUNT *Fees Earned* ACCOUNT NO. *41*

DATE		ITEM	POST. REF.	DEBIT	CREDIT	BALANCE	
						DEBIT	CREDIT

ACCOUNT *Salary Expense* ACCOUNT NO. *51*

DATE		ITEM	POST. REF.	DEBIT	CREDIT	BALANCE	
						DEBIT	CREDIT

ACCOUNT *Rent Expense* ACCOUNT NO.

DATE		ITEM	POST. REF.	DEBIT	CREDIT	BALANCE	
						DEBIT	CREDIT

ACCOUNT *Supplies Expense* ACCOUNT NO.

DATE		ITEM	POST. REF.	DEBIT	CREDIT	BALANCE	
						DEBIT	CREDIT

Name ______________________________

PROBLEM 4-5 ___, Continued

ACCOUNT *Depreciation Expense* ACCOUNT NO. *54*

DATE		ITEM	POST. REF.	DEBIT	CREDIT	BALANCE DEBIT	BALANCE CREDIT

ACCOUNT *Insurance Expense* ACCOUNT NO. *55*

DATE		ITEM	POST. REF.	DEBIT	CREDIT	BALANCE DEBIT	BALANCE CREDIT

ACCOUNT *Miscellaneous Expense* ACCOUNT NO. *59*

DATE		ITEM	POST. REF.	DEBIT	CREDIT	BALANCE DEBIT	BALANCE CREDIT

PROBLEM 4-5 ___, Continued

3.

Unadjusted Trial Balance

PROBLEM 4-5 ___, Continued

5. Optional (Appendix)

	A	B	C	D	E	F	G	H	I	J	K
1											
2	End-of-Period Spreadsheet (Work Sheet)										
3											
4		Unadjusted				Adjusted		Income		Balance	
5		Trial Balance		Adjustments		Trial Balance		Statement		Sheet	
6	Account Title	Dr.	Cr.	Dr.	Cr.	Dr.	Cr.	Dr.	Cr.	Dr.	Cr.
7											
8											
9											
10											
11											
12											
13											
14											
15											
16											
17											
18											
19											
20											
21											
22											
23											
24											
25											
26											
27											
28											
29											
30											

PROBLEM 4-5 ___, Continued

6.

JOURNAL

PAGE *3*

DATE		DESCRIPTION	POST. REF.	DEBIT	CREDIT
		Adjusting Entries			

Name ______________________________

PROBLEM 4-5 ___, Continued

7.

Adjusted Trial Balance

PROBLEM 4-5 ___, Continued

8.

Income Statement

Statement of Owner's Equity

PROBLEM 4-5 ___, Continued

Balance Sheet

PROBLEM 4-5 ___, Continued

9.

JOURNAL

PAGE *4*

DATE		DESCRIPTION	POST. REF.	DEBIT	CREDIT
		Closing Entries			

Name ______________________________

PROBLEM 4-5 ___, Concluded

10.

Post-Closing Trial Balance

This Page Not Used.

CONTINUING PROBLEM

1. Optional (Appendix)

	A	B	C	D	E	F	G	H	I	J	
1											K
2	**End-of-Period Spreadsheet (Work Sheet)**										
3											
4		**Unadjusted Trial Balance**		**Adjustments**		**Adjusted Trial Balance**		**Income Statement**		**Balance Sheet**	
5											
6	**Account Title**	**Dr.**	**Cr.**	**Dr.**	**Cr.**	**Dr.**	**Cr.**	**Dr.**	**Cr.**	**Dr.**	**Cr.**
7											
8											
9											
10											
11											
12											
13											
14											
15											
16											
17											
18											
19											
20											
21											
22											
23											
24											
25											
26											
27											
28											
29											
30											
31											
32											

CONTINUING PROBLEM, Continued

2.

Income Statement

Statement of Owner's Equity

Name ______________________________

CONTINUING PROBLEM, Continued

Balance Sheet

CONTINUING PROBLEM, Continued

3. Note: Use the general ledger accounts provided in Chapter 3, page 118–124.

JOURNAL

PAGE 4

	DATE		DESCRIPTION	POST. REF.	DEBIT	CREDIT	
1			*Closing Entries*				1
2							2
3							3
4							4
5							5
6							6
7							7
8							8
9							9
10							10
11							11
12							12
13							13
14							14
15							15
16							16
17							17
18							18
19							19
20							20
21							21
22							22
23							23
24							24
25							25
26							26
27							27
28							28
29							29
30							30
31							31
32							32
33							33
34							34

Name ______________________________

CONTINUING PROBLEM, Concluded

4.

Post-Closing Trial Balance

This Page Not Used.

Name ______________________________

COMPREHENSIVE PROBLEM 1

1. and 2.

JOURNAL

PAGE 5

DATE		DESCRIPTION	POST. REF.	DEBIT	CREDIT

COMPREHENSIVE PROBLEM 1, Continued

JOURNAL

PAGE 6

DATE		DESCRIPTION	POST. REF.	DEBIT	CREDIT

Name ______________________________

COMPREHENSIVE PROBLEM 1, Continued

2., 6., and 9.

GENERAL LEDGER

ACCOUNT *Cash* ACCOUNT NO. *11*

DATE		ITEM	POST. REF.	DEBIT	CREDIT	BALANCE	
						DEBIT	CREDIT

ACCOUNT *Accounts Receivable* ACCOUNT NO. *12*

DATE		ITEM	POST. REF.	DEBIT	CREDIT	BALANCE	
						DEBIT	CREDIT

COMPREHENSIVE PROBLEM 1, Continued

ACCOUNT *Supplies* ACCOUNT NO. *14*

DATE		ITEM	POST. REF.	DEBIT	CREDIT	BALANCE	
						DEBIT	CREDIT

ACCOUNT *Prepaid Rent* ACCOUNT NO. *15*

DATE		ITEM	POST. REF.	DEBIT	CREDIT	BALANCE	
						DEBIT	CREDIT

ACCOUNT *Prepaid Insurance* ACCOUNT NO. *16*

DATE		ITEM	POST. REF.	DEBIT	CREDIT	BALANCE	
						DEBIT	CREDIT

ACCOUNT *Office Equipment* ACCOUNT NO. *18*

DATE		ITEM	POST. REF.	DEBIT	CREDIT	BALANCE	
						DEBIT	CREDIT

ACCOUNT *Accumulated Depreciation—Office Equipment* ACCOUNT NO. *19*

DATE		ITEM	POST. REF.	DEBIT	CREDIT	BALANCE	
						DEBIT	CREDIT

Name ______________________________

COMPREHENSIVE PROBLEM 1, Continued

ACCOUNT *Accounts Payable* ACCOUNT NO. *21*

DATE		ITEM	POST. REF.	DEBIT	CREDIT	BALANCE	
						DEBIT	CREDIT

ACCOUNT *Salaries Payable* ACCOUNT NO. *22*

DATE		ITEM	POST. REF.	DEBIT	CREDIT	BALANCE	
						DEBIT	CREDIT

ACCOUNT *Unearned Fees* ACCOUNT NO. *23*

DATE		ITEM	POST. REF.	DEBIT	CREDIT	BALANCE	
						DEBIT	CREDIT

ACCOUNT *Kelly Pitney, Capital* ACCOUNT NO. *31*

DATE		ITEM	POST. REF.	DEBIT	CREDIT	BALANCE	
						DEBIT	CREDIT

COMPREHENSIVE PROBLEM 1, Continued

ACCOUNT *Kelly Pitney, Drawing* ACCOUNT NO. *32*

DATE		ITEM	POST. REF.	DEBIT	CREDIT	BALANCE DEBIT	BALANCE CREDIT

ACCOUNT *Fees Earned* ACCOUNT NO. *41*

DATE		ITEM	POST. REF.	DEBIT	CREDIT	BALANCE DEBIT	BALANCE CREDIT

ACCOUNT *Salary Expense* ACCOUNT NO. *51*

DATE		ITEM	POST. REF.	DEBIT	CREDIT	BALANCE DEBIT	BALANCE CREDIT

ACCOUNT *Rent Expense* ACCOUNT NO. *52*

DATE		ITEM	POST. REF.	DEBIT	CREDIT	BALANCE DEBIT	BALANCE CREDIT

Name ______________________________

COMPREHENSIVE PROBLEM 1, Continued

ACCOUNT *Supplies Expense* ACCOUNT NO. *53*

DATE		ITEM	POST. REF.	DEBIT	CREDIT	BALANCE	
						DEBIT	CREDIT

ACCOUNT *Depreciation Expense* ACCOUNT NO. *54*

DATE		ITEM	POST. REF.	DEBIT	CREDIT	BALANCE	
						DEBIT	CREDIT

ACCOUNT *Insurance Expense* ACCOUNT NO. *55*

DATE		ITEM	POST. REF.	DEBIT	CREDIT	BALANCE	
						DEBIT	CREDIT

ACCOUNT *Miscellaneous Expense* ACCOUNT NO. *59*

DATE		ITEM	POST. REF.	DEBIT	CREDIT	BALANCE	
						DEBIT	CREDIT

COMPREHENSIVE PROBLEM 1, Continued

3.

Unadjusted Trial Balance

COMPREHENSIVE PROBLEM 1, Continued

5. Optional (Appendix)

	A	B	C	D	E	F	G	H	I	J	K
1											
2	End-of-Period Spreadsheet (Work Sheet)										
3											
4		Unadjusted				Adjusted		Income		Balance	
5		Trial Balance		Adjustments		Trial Balance		Statement		Sheet	
6	Account Title	Dr.	Cr.	Dr.	Cr.	Dr.	Cr.	Dr.	Cr.	Dr.	Cr.
7											
8											
9											
10											
11											
12											
13											
14											
15											
16											
17											
18											
19											
20											
21											
22											
23											
24											
25											
26											
27											
28											
29											
30											

COMPREHENSIVE PROBLEM 1, Continued

6.

JOURNAL

PAGE 7

	DATE		DESCRIPTION	POST. REF.	DEBIT	CREDIT	
1			*Adjusting Entries*				1
2							2
3							3
4							4
5							5
6							6
7							7
8							8
9							9
10							10
11							11
12							12
13							13
14							14
15							15
16							16
17							17
18							18
19							19
20							20
21							21
22							22
23							23
24							24
25							25
26							26
27							27
28							28
29							29
30							30
31							31
32							32
33							33
34							34

Name ______________________________

COMPREHENSIVE PROBLEM 1, Continued

7.

Adjusted Trial Balance

COMPREHENSIVE PROBLEM 1, Continued

8.

Income Statement

Statement of Owner's Equity

COMPREHENSIVE PROBLEM 1, Continued

Balance Sheet

COMPREHENSIVE PROBLEM 1, Continued

9.

JOURNAL

PAGE *8*

DATE		DESCRIPTION	POST. REF.	DEBIT	CREDIT
		Closing Entries			

Name ______________________________

COMPREHENSIVE PROBLEM 1, Concluded

10.

Post-Closing Trial Balance

This Page Not Used.

Name ______________________________

EXERCISE 5-1

REVENUE JOURNAL

Date	Invoice No.	Account Debited	Post. Ref.	Accounts Rec. Dr. Fees Earned Cr.
20Y3 May 1	112	Hazmat Safety Co.	(a) ________	$2,050
10	113	Masco Co.	(b) ________	980
20	114	Alpha GenCorp	(c) ________	2,800
27	115	Tillman Inc.	(d) ________	1,240
31				$7,070
				(e) ________

EXERCISE 5-2

a., b., and c.

Accounts Receivable

Alpha GenCorp

Hazmat Safety Co.

Masco Co.

Tillman Inc.

Name ______________________________

EXERCISE 5-2, Concluded

d.

Account Receivable Customer Balances

EXERCISE 5-3

a. Receipt of cash refund from overpayment of taxes: ______________________________

b. Adjustment to record accrued salaries at the end of the year: ______________________________

c. Providing services on account: ______________________________

d. Investment of additional cash in the business by the owner: ______________________________

e. Receipt of cash on account from a customer: ______________________________

f. Receipt of cash for rent: ______________________________

g. Receipt of cash from sale of office equipment: ______________________________

h. Sale of used office equipment on account, at cost, to a neighboring business: ______________________________

____

i. Closing of drawing account at the end of the year: ______________________________

j. Providing services for cash: ______________________________

EXERCISE 5-4

a. Payment of six months' rent in advance: ______________________________

b. Purchase of an office computer on account: ______________________________

c. Purchase of office supplies on account: ______________________________

d. Adjustment to record depreciation at the end of the month: ______________________________

e. Adjustment to record accrued salaries at the end of the period: ______________________________

f. Purchase of services on account: ______________________________

g. Adjustment to prepaid rent at the end of the month: ______________________________

h. Purchase of office equipment for cash: ______________________________

i. Adjustment to prepaid insurance at the end of the month: ______________________________

j. Purchase of office supplies for cash: ______________________________

k. Advance payment of a one-year fire insurance policy on the office: ______________________________

EXERCISE 5-5

Apr. 3

Apr. 6

Apr. 24

EXERCISE 5-6

a.

REVENUE JOURNAL

PAGE

	DATE		INVOICE NO.	ACCOUNT DEBITED	POST. REF.	ACCTS. REC. DR. FEES EARNED CR.	
1							1
2							2
3							3
4							4
5							5
6							6
7							7
8							8
9							9
10							10

b.

c.

Name ______________________________

EXERCISE 5-7

a. and b.

Aladdin Co.

Clearmark Co.

Life Star Inc.

c.

Accounts Receivable

Fees Earned

EXERCISE 5-7, Concluded

d.

Accounts Receivable Customer Balances

e. ____

EXERCISE 5-8

Accounts Receivable Customer Balances

Name ______________________________

EXERCISE 5-8, Concluded

Accounts Receivable

(Controlling)

EXERCISE 5-9

REVENUE JOURNAL

PAGE 8

	DATE		INVOICE NO.	ACCOUNT DEBITED	POST. REF.	ACCTS. REC. DR. FEES EARNED CR.	
1							1
2							2
3							3
4							4
5							5
6							6
7							7
8							8
9							9
10							10

CASH RECEIPTS JOURNAL

PAGE 12

	DATE		ACCOUNT CREDITED	POST. REF.	FEES EARNED CR.	ACCOUNTS REC. CR.	CASH DR.	
1								1
2								2
3								3
4								4
5								5
6								6
7								7
8								8
9								9
10								10

EXERCISE 5-10

a.

REVENUE JOURNAL

PAGE 19

	DATE		INVOICE NO.	ACCOUNT DEBITED	POST. REF.	ACCTS. REC. DR. FEES EARNED CR.	
1							1
2							2
3							3
4							4
5							5
6							6
7							7
8							8
9							9
10							10

CASH RECEIPTS JOURNAL

PAGE 25

	DATE		ACCOUNT CREDITED	POST. REF.	FEES EARNED CR.	ACCOUNTS REC. CR.	CASH DR.	
1								1
2								2
3								3
4								4
5								5
6								6
7								7
8								8
9								9
10								10

Name ______________________________

EXERCISE 5-10, Concluded

b.

Accounts Receivable Customer Balances

Accounts Receivable

c. ______________________________

EXERCISE 5-11

a. ______________________

b. ______________________

c. ______________________

d. ______________________

e. ______________________

f. ______________________

g. ______________________

h. ______________________

i. ______________________

j. ______________________

k. ______________________

l. ______________________

m. ______________________

EXERCISE 5-12

a. ______________________

b. ______________________

c. ______________________

d. ______________________

e. ______________________

f. ______________________

g. ______________________

h. ______________________

i. ______________________

j. ______________________

k. ______________________

l. ______________________

Name ______________________________

EXERCISE 5-13

June 6 ______________________________

____

____

____

June 14 ______________________________

____

____

____

June 16 ______________________________

____

____

____

Name ______________________

EXERCISE 5-14

a.

PURCHASES JOURNAL

	DATE		ACCOUNT CREDITED	POST. REF.	ACCOUNTS PAYABLE CR.	OFFICE SUPPLIES DR.	OTHER ACCOUNTS DR.	POST. REF.	AMOUNT	
1										1
2										2
3										3
4										4
5										5
6										6
7										7
8										8
9										9

b. ______________________

c. ______________________

EXERCISE 5-15

a. and b.

Enviro-Wash Supplies Inc.

Nicely Co.

Office Mate Inc.

c.

Accounts Payable

Cleaning Supplies

EXERCISE 5-15, Concluded

d.

Accounts Payable Creditor Balances

e. ____

Name ______________________________

EXERCISE 5-16

Accounts Payable Creditor Balances	

Accounts Payable (Controlling)	

Name ______________________

EXERCISE 5-17

PURCHASES JOURNAL

PAGE *36*

	DATE	ACCOUNT CREDITED	POST. REF.	ACCOUNTS PAYABLE CR.	CLEANING SUPPLIES DR.	OTHER ACCOUNTS DR.	POST. REF.	AMOUNT	
1									1
2									2
3									3
4									4
5									5
6									6
7									7
8									8
9									9

CASH PAYMENTS JOURNAL

PAGE *41*

	DATE	CK. NO.	ACCOUNT DEBITED	POST. REF.	OTHER ACCOUNTS DR.	ACCOUNTS PAYABLE DR.	CASH CR.	
1								1
2								2
3								3
4								4
5								5
6								6
7								7
8								8
9								9

EXERCISE 5-18

a.

PURCHASES JOURNAL

PAGE 16

	DATE		ACCOUNT CREDITED	POST. REF.	ACCOUNTS PAYABLE CR.	PET SUPPLIES DR.	OTHER ACCOUNTS DR.	POST. REF.	AMOUNT	
1										1
2										2
3										3
4										4
5										5
6										6
7										7
8										8

CASH PAYMENTS JOURNAL

PAGE 22

	DATE		CK. NO.	ACCOUNT DEBITED	POST. REF.	OTHER ACCOUNTS DR.	ACCOUNTS PAYABLE DR.	CASH CR.	
1									1
2									2
3									3
4									4
5									5
6									6
7									7
8									8
9									9

EXERCISE 5-18, Concluded

b.

Accounts Payable Creditor Balances

Accounts Payable

c. ______________________

Name ______________________________

EXERCISE 5-19

a. ______________________________

b.

Accounts Payable Creditor Balances

EXERCISE 5-20

a. ______________________________

b. ______________________________

c. ______________________________

d. ______________________________

e. ______________________________

EXERCISE 5-21

EXERCISE 5-22

a.

b.

Name ______________________

EXERCISE 5-22, Concluded

c.

EXERCISE 5-23

a. ______________________

b.

JOURNAL PAGE

	DATE		DESCRIPTION	POST. REF.	DEBIT	CREDIT	
1							1
2							2
3							3
4							4

c. ______________________

d. ______________________

e. ______________________

Name ______________________________

EXERCISE 5-24

a. Amazon.com: ______________________________

____

b. Dell Inc.: ______________________________

____

c. DuPont: ______________________________

____

d. Intuit Inc.: ______________________________

____

e. L.L. Bean, Inc.: ______________________________

____

f. W.W. Grainger, Inc.: ______________________________

____

EXERCISE 5-25

a.

	RECENT YEAR (IN MILLIONS)	PRIOR YEAR (IN MILLIONS)	INCREASE (DECREASE)	
			AMOUNT	PERCENT

b.

	RECENT YEAR		PRIOR YEAR	
	AMOUNT	PERCENT	AMOUNT	PERCENT

EXERCISE 5-25, Concluded

c. ________________________

Name ______________________________

EXERCISE 5-26

a.

MAJOR PRODUCT SEGMENTS	FOR A RECENT YEAR (IN MILLIONS)	PERCENT

b. ______________________________

EXERCISE 5-27

a.

	YEAR 2 (IN MILLIONS)	YEAR 1 (IN MILLIONS)	INCREASE (DECREASE)	
			AMOUNT	PERCENT

b.

	YEAR 2		YEAR 1	
	AMOUNT (IN MILLIONS)	PERCENT	AMOUNT (IN MILLIONS)	PERCENT

c. ______________________________

Name ________________________________

PROBLEM 5-1 ___

1. and 2.

REVENUE JOURNAL

PAGE 1

	DATE		INVOICE NO.	ACCOUNT DEBITED	POST. REF.	ACCTS. REC. DR. FEES EARNED CR.	
1							1
2							2
3							3
4							4
5							5
6							6
7							7
8							8
9							9
10							10
11							11

JOURNAL

PAGE 1

	DATE		DESCRIPTION	POST. REF.	DEBIT	CREDIT	
1							1
2							2
3							3
4							4

PROBLEM 5-1 ___, Continued

ACCOUNTS RECEIVABLE SUBSIDIARY LEDGER

NAME

DATE		ITEM	POST. REF.	DEBIT	CREDIT	BALANCE

NAME

DATE		ITEM	POST. REF.	DEBIT	CREDIT	BALANCE

NAME

DATE		ITEM	POST. REF.	DEBIT	CREDIT	BALANCE

NAME

DATE		ITEM	POST. REF.	DEBIT	CREDIT	BALANCE

NAME

DATE		ITEM	POST. REF.	DEBIT	CREDIT	BALANCE

PROBLEM 5-1 ___, Concluded

2.

GENERAL LEDGER

ACCOUNT ______________________ ACCOUNT NO.

DATE		ITEM	POST. REF.	DEBIT	CREDIT	BALANCE DEBIT	BALANCE CREDIT

ACCOUNT ______________________ ACCOUNT NO.

DATE		ITEM	POST. REF.	DEBIT	CREDIT	BALANCE DEBIT	BALANCE CREDIT

ACCOUNT ______________________ ACCOUNT NO.

DATE		ITEM	POST. REF.	DEBIT	CREDIT	BALANCE DEBIT	BALANCE CREDIT

3. a. ______________________________

b. ______________________________

4. ______________________________

This Page Not Used.

Name ____________________

PROBLEM 5-2 ___

1. and 5.

GENERAL LEDGER

ACCOUNT ACCOUNT NO.

DATE		ITEM	POST. REF.	DEBIT	CREDIT	BALANCE DEBIT	BALANCE CREDIT

ACCOUNT ACCOUNT NO.

DATE		ITEM	POST. REF.	DEBIT	CREDIT	BALANCE DEBIT	BALANCE CREDIT

ACCOUNT ACCOUNT NO.

DATE		ITEM	POST. REF.	DEBIT	CREDIT	BALANCE DEBIT	BALANCE CREDIT

ACCOUNT ACCOUNT NO.

DATE		ITEM	POST. REF.	DEBIT	CREDIT	BALANCE DEBIT	BALANCE CREDIT

PROBLEM 5-2 ___, Continued

2. and 4.

ACCOUNTS RECEIVABLE SUBSIDIARY LEDGER

NAME

DATE		ITEM	POST. REF.	DEBIT	CREDIT	BALANCE

NAME

DATE		ITEM	POST. REF.	DEBIT	CREDIT	BALANCE

NAME

DATE		ITEM	POST. REF.	DEBIT	CREDIT	BALANCE

NAME

DATE		ITEM	POST. REF.	DEBIT	CREDIT	BALANCE

Name ____________________

PROBLEM 5-2 ___, Continued

3., 4., and 5.

REVENUE JOURNAL

PAGE *40*

DATE		INVOICE NO.	ACCOUNT DEBITED	POST. REF.	ACCTS. REC. DR. FEES EARNED CR.

CASH RECEIPTS JOURNAL

PAGE *36*

DATE		ACCOUNT CREDITED	POST. REF.	FEES EARNED CR.	ACCOUNTS REC. CR.	CASH DR.

JOURNAL

PAGE *1*

DATE		DESCRIPTION	POST. REF.	DEBIT	CREDIT

PROBLEM 5-2 ___, Concluded

6. ______________________________

7. ______________________________

Name ______________________________

PROBLEM 5-3 ___

1. and 4.

GENERAL LEDGER

ACCOUNT *Field Supplies* ACCOUNT NO. *14*

DATE		ITEM	POST. REF.	DEBIT	CREDIT	BALANCE	
						DEBIT	CREDIT

ACCOUNT *Office Supplies* ACCOUNT NO. *15*

DATE		ITEM	POST. REF.	DEBIT	CREDIT	BALANCE	
						DEBIT	CREDIT

ACCOUNT *Office Equipment* ACCOUNT NO. *18*

DATE		ITEM	POST. REF.	DEBIT	CREDIT	BALANCE	
						DEBIT	CREDIT

ACCOUNT *Accounts Payable* ACCOUNT NO. *21*

DATE		ITEM	POST. REF.	DEBIT	CREDIT	BALANCE	
						DEBIT	CREDIT

PROBLEM 5-3 ___, Continued

2. and 3.

ACCOUNTS PAYABLE SUBSIDIARY LEDGER

NAME

DATE		ITEM	POST. REF.	DEBIT	CREDIT	BALANCE

NAME

DATE		ITEM	POST. REF.	DEBIT	CREDIT	BALANCE

NAME

DATE		ITEM	POST. REF.	DEBIT	CREDIT	BALANCE

NAME

DATE		ITEM	POST. REF.	DEBIT	CREDIT	BALANCE

Name ________________________________

PROBLEM 5-3 ___, Continued

NAME

DATE		ITEM	POST. REF.	DEBIT	CREDIT	BALANCE

Name ______________________

PROBLEM 5-3 ___, Concluded

3. and 4.

PURCHASES JOURNAL

PAGE *30*

	DATE		ACCOUNT CREDITED	POST. REF.	ACCOUNTS PAYABLE CR.	FIELD SUPPLIES DR.	OFFICE SUPPLIES DR.	OTHER ACCOUNTS DR.	POST. REF.	AMOUNT	
1											1
2											2
3											3
4											4
5											5
6											6
7											7
8											8
9											9
10											10
11											11
12											12
13											13
14											14
15											15

5. a. ______________________

b. ______________________

6. ______________________

____

Name ______________________________

PROBLEM 5-4 ___

., 2., and 3.

PURCHASES JOURNAL

PAGE *1*

	DATE		ACCOUNT CREDITED	POST. REF.	ACCOUNTS PAYABLE CR.	FIELD SUPPLIES DR.	OFFICE SUPPLIES DR.	OTHER ACCOUNTS DR.	POST. REF.	AMOUNT	
1											1
2											2
3											3
4											4
5											5
6											6
7											7
8											8
9											9
10											10
11											11
12											12
13											13
14											14
15											15
16											16
17											17
18											18
19											19
20											20

PROBLEM 5-4 ___, Continued

CASH PAYMENTS JOURNAL

PAGE 1

	DATE		CK. NO.	ACCOUNT DEBITED	POST. REF.	OTHER ACCOUNTS DR.	ACCOUNTS PAYABLE DR.	CASH CR.	
1									1
2									2
3									3
4									4
5									5
6									6
7									7
8									8
9									9
10									10
11									11
12									12
13									13
14									14
15									15

1. and 2.

JOURNAL

PAGE 1

	DATE		DESCRIPTION	POST. REF.	DEBIT	CREDIT	
1							1
2							2
3							3
4							4
5							5

PROBLEM 5-4 ___, Continued

1.

ACCOUNTS PAYABLE SUBSIDIARY LEDGER

NAME

DATE		ITEM	POST. REF.	DEBIT	CREDIT	BALANCE

NAME

DATE		ITEM	POST. REF.	DEBIT	CREDIT	BALANCE

NAME

DATE		ITEM	POST. REF.	DEBIT	CREDIT	BALANCE

PROBLEM 5-4 ___, Continued

2. and 3.

GENERAL LEDGER

ACCOUNT ACCOUNT NO.

DATE		ITEM	POST. REF.	DEBIT	CREDIT	BALANCE	
						DEBIT	CREDIT

ACCOUNT ACCOUNT NO.

DATE		ITEM	POST. REF.	DEBIT	CREDIT	BALANCE	
						DEBIT	CREDIT

ACCOUNT ACCOUNT NO.

DATE		ITEM	POST. REF.	DEBIT	CREDIT	BALANCE	
						DEBIT	CREDIT

ACCOUNT ACCOUNT NO.

DATE		ITEM	POST. REF.	DEBIT	CREDIT	BALANCE	
						DEBIT	CREDIT

ACCOUNT ACCOUNT NO.

DATE		ITEM	POST. REF.	DEBIT	CREDIT	BALANCE	
						DEBIT	CREDIT

Name ______________________________

PROBLEM 5-4 ___, Continued

ACCOUNT ACCOUNT NO.

DATE		ITEM	POST. REF.	DEBIT	CREDIT	BALANCE DEBIT	BALANCE CREDIT

ACCOUNT ACCOUNT NO.

DATE		ITEM	POST. REF.	DEBIT	CREDIT	BALANCE DEBIT	BALANCE CREDIT

ACCOUNT ACCOUNT NO.

DATE		ITEM	POST. REF.	DEBIT	CREDIT	BALANCE DEBIT	BALANCE CREDIT

ACCOUNT ACCOUNT NO.

DATE		ITEM	POST. REF.	DEBIT	CREDIT	BALANCE DEBIT	BALANCE CREDIT

ACCOUNT ACCOUNT NO.

DATE		ITEM	POST. REF.	DEBIT	CREDIT	BALANCE DEBIT	BALANCE CREDIT

PROBLEM 5-4 ___, Concluded

4.

Accounts Payable Creditor Balances

5. ______________________________

Name ______________________________

PROBLEM 5-5 ___

1., 3., and 4.

GENERAL LEDGER

ACCOUNT *Cash* ACCOUNT NO. *11*

DATE		ITEM	POST. REF.	DEBIT	CREDIT	BALANCE DEBIT	BALANCE CREDIT

ACCOUNT *Accounts Receivable* ACCOUNT NO. *12*

DATE		ITEM	POST. REF.	DEBIT	CREDIT	BALANCE DEBIT	BALANCE CREDIT

ACCOUNT *Maintenance Supplies* ACCOUNT NO. *14*

DATE		ITEM	POST. REF.	DEBIT	CREDIT	BALANCE DEBIT	BALANCE CREDIT

ACCOUNT *Office Supplies* ACCOUNT NO. *15*

DATE		ITEM	POST. REF.	DEBIT	CREDIT	BALANCE DEBIT	BALANCE CREDIT

PROBLEM 5-5 ___, Continued

ACCOUNT *Office Equipment* ACCOUNT NO. *16*

DATE		ITEM	POST. REF.	DEBIT	CREDIT	BALANCE DEBIT	BALANCE CREDIT

ACCOUNT *Accumulated Depreciation—Office Equipment* ACCOUNT NO. *17*

DATE		ITEM	POST. REF.	DEBIT	CREDIT	BALANCE DEBIT	BALANCE CREDIT

ACCOUNT *Vehicles* ACCOUNT NO. *18*

DATE		ITEM	POST. REF.	DEBIT	CREDIT	BALANCE DEBIT	BALANCE CREDIT

ACCOUNT *Accumulated Depreciation—Vehicles* ACCOUNT NO. *19*

DATE		ITEM	POST. REF.	DEBIT	CREDIT	BALANCE DEBIT	BALANCE CREDIT

ACCOUNT *Accounts Payable* ACCOUNT NO. *21*

DATE		ITEM	POST. REF.	DEBIT	CREDIT	BALANCE DEBIT	BALANCE CREDIT

Name ______________________________

PROBLEM 5-5 ___, Continued

ACCOUNT ______________________, *Capital* ACCOUNT NO. *31*

DATE		ITEM	POST. REF.	DEBIT	CREDIT	BALANCE	
						DEBIT	CREDIT

ACCOUNT ______________________, *Drawing* ACCOUNT NO. *32*

DATE		ITEM	POST. REF.	DEBIT	CREDIT	BALANCE	
						DEBIT	CREDIT

ACCOUNT *Fees Earned* ACCOUNT NO. *41*

DATE		ITEM	POST. REF.	DEBIT	CREDIT	BALANCE	
						DEBIT	CREDIT

ACCOUNT *Rent Revenue* ACCOUNT NO. *42*

DATE		ITEM	POST. REF.	DEBIT	CREDIT	BALANCE	
						DEBIT	CREDIT

(This account is not used in Problem 5-5A.)

ACCOUNT *Driver Salaries Expense* ACCOUNT NO. *51*

DATE		ITEM	POST. REF.	DEBIT	CREDIT	BALANCE	
						DEBIT	CREDIT

PROBLEM 5-5 ___, Continued

ACCOUNT *Maintenance Supplies Expense* ACCOUNT NO. *52*

DATE		ITEM	POST. REF.	DEBIT	CREDIT	BALANCE	
						DEBIT	CREDIT

ACCOUNT *Fuel Expense* ACCOUNT NO. *53*

DATE		ITEM	POST. REF.	DEBIT	CREDIT	BALANCE	
						DEBIT	CREDIT

ACCOUNT *Office Salaries Expense* ACCOUNT NO. *61*

DATE		ITEM	POST. REF.	DEBIT	CREDIT	BALANCE	
						DEBIT	CREDIT

ACCOUNT *Rent Expense* ACCOUNT NO. *62*

DATE		ITEM	POST. REF.	DEBIT	CREDIT	BALANCE	
						DEBIT	CREDIT

ACCOUNT *Advertising Expense* ACCOUNT NO. *63*

DATE		ITEM	POST. REF.	DEBIT	CREDIT	BALANCE	
						DEBIT	CREDIT

ACCOUNT *Miscellaneous Administrative Expense* ACCOUNT NO. *64*

DATE		ITEM	POST. REF.	DEBIT	CREDIT	BALANCE	
						DEBIT	CREDIT

PROBLEM 5-5 ___, Continued
2. and 4.

PURCHASES JOURNAL

PAGE 37

	DATE		ACCOUNT CREDITED	POST. REF.	ACCOUNTS PAYABLE CR.	MAINTENANCE SUPPLIES DR.	OFFICE SUPPLIES DR.	OTHER ACCOUNTS DR.	POST. REF.	AMOUNT	
1											1
2											2
3											3
4											4
5											5
6											6
7											7
8											8
9											9
10											10
11											11
12											12
13											13
14											14
15											15
16											16
17											17
18											18
19											19
20											20

PROBLEM 5-5 ___, Continued

CASH RECEIPTS JOURNAL

PAGE *31*

	DATE		ACCOUNT CREDITED	POST. REF.	OTHER ACCOUNTS CR.	ACCOUNTS REC. CR.	CASH DR.	
1								1
2								2
3								3
4								4
5								5
6								6
7								7
8								8
9								9
10								10
11								11
12								12
13								13
14								14
15								15
16								16

REVENUE JOURNAL

PAGE *35*

	DATE		INVOICE NO.	ACCOUNT DEBITED	POST. REF.	ACCTS. REC. DR. FEES EARNED CR.	
1							1
2							2
3							3
4							4
5							5
6							6
7							7
8							8
9							9
10							10
11							11
12							12
13							13
14							14

Name ______________________________

PROBLEM 5-5 ___, Continued

CASH PAYMENTS JOURNAL

PAGE 34

	DATE		CK. NO.	ACCOUNT DEBITED	POST. REF.	OTHER ACCOUNTS DR.	ACCOUNTS PAYABLE DR.	CASH CR.	
1									1
2									2
3									3
4									4
5									5
6									6
7									7
8									8
9									9
10									10
11									11
12									12
13									13
14									14
15									15
16									16
17									17
18									18
19									19
20									20
21									21
22									22
23									23
24									24

3.

JOURNAL

PAGE 1

	DATE		DESCRIPTION	POST. REF.	DEBIT	CREDIT	
1							1
2							2
3							3
4							4
5							5

PROBLEM 5-5 ___, Concluded

5.

Unadjusted Trial Balance

Name ______________________________

EXERCISE 6-1

a. ______________________________

b. ______________________________

c. ______________________________

EXERCISE 6-2

EXERCISE 6-3

Balance Sheet Accounts

Acct. #	Account Name

Income Statement Accounts

Acct. #	Account Name

Name ______________________________

EXERCISE 6-4

a. ______________________________

____

____

b. ______________________________

EXERCISE 6-5

____

____

EXERCISE 6-6

(1) ______________________________

____

____

(2) ______________________________

____

____

(3) ______________________________

____

____

(4) ______________________________

____

____

EXERCISE 6-7

JOURNAL

PAGE

	DATE		DESCRIPTION	POST. REF.	DEBIT	CREDIT	
1							1
2							2
3							3
4							4
5							5
6							6
7							7
8							8
9							9
10							10
11							11
12							12

EXERCISE 6-8

JOURNAL

PAGE

	DATE		DESCRIPTION	POST. REF.	DEBIT	CREDIT	
1							1
2							2
3							3
4							4
5							5
6							6
7							7
8							8
9							9
10							10
11							11
12							12
13							13
14							14
15							15
16							16
17							17
18							18
19							19
20							20
21							21
22							22
23							23
24							24

EXERCISE 6-9

JOURNAL

PAGE

DATE	DESCRIPTION	POST. REF.	DEBIT	CREDIT

Name ______________________

EXERCISE 6-10

a. ______________________

b.

JOURNAL PAGE

	DATE		DESCRIPTION	POST. REF.	DEBIT	CREDIT	
1							1
2							2
3							3
4							4
5							5
6							6
7							7
8							8
9							9

EXERCISE 6-11

(1) ______________________

(2) ______________________

(3) ______________________

(4) ______________________

(5) ______________________

EXERCISE 6-12

a. Amount of the sale: ______________________

b. Amount debited to Accounts Receivable: ______________________

c. Amount received within the discount period: ______________________

EXERCISE 6-13

	Merchandise	Freight Paid by Seller		Customer Returns and Allowances	Amount to be Paid in Full
a.	$14,000	—	FOB destination, n/30	$3,250	$__________
b.	21,200	$380	FOB shipping point, 2/10, n/30	4,000	$__________
c.	16,400	—	FOB shipping point, 1/10, n/30	900	$__________
d.	7,500	250	FOB shipping point, 2/10, n/30	1,200	$__________
e.	28,800	—	FOB destination, 1/10, n/30	—	$__________

EXERCISE 6-14

JOURNAL

PAGE

	DATE		DESCRIPTION	POST. REF.	DEBIT	CREDIT	
1							1
2							2
3							3
4							4
5							5
6							6
7							7
8							8
9							9
10							10
11							11
12							12
13							13
14							14
15							15
16							16
17							17
18							18
19							19
20							20
21							21
22							22
23							23
24							24

Name ______________________________

EXERCISE 6-15

JOURNAL PAGE

	DATE		DESCRIPTION	POST. REF.	DEBIT	CREDIT	
1							1
2							2
3							3
4							4
5							5
6							6
7							7
8							8
9							9
10							10
11							11
12							12
13							13
14							14

EXERCISE 6-16

a. ______________________________

b. ______________________________

c. ______________________________

d. ______________________________

EXERCISE 6-17

JOURNAL

PAGE

	DATE		DESCRIPTION	POST. REF.	DEBIT	CREDIT	
1							1
2							2
3							3
4							4
5							5
6							6
7							7
8							8
9							9
10							10
11							11
12							12
13							13
14							14

EXERCISE 6-18

	Debit	Credit
a. Cost of Merchandise Sold	______	______
b. Customer Refunds Payable	______	______
c. Delivery Expense.......................................	______	______
d. Estimated Returns Inventory	______	______
e. Merchandise Inventory	______	______
f. Sales...	______	______
g. Sales Tax Payable......................................	______	______

Name ______________________________

EXERCISE 6-19

JOURNAL PAGE

	DATE		DESCRIPTION	POST. REF.	DEBIT	CREDIT	
1							1
2							2
3							3
4							4
5							5
6							6
7							7

EXERCISE 6-20

a. and b.

JOURNAL PAGE

	DATE		DESCRIPTION	POST. REF.	DEBIT	CREDIT	
1							1
2							2
3							3
4							4
5							5
6							6
7							7
8							8
9							9
10							10
11							11
12							12

EXERCISE 6-21

a. and b.

JOURNAL

PAGE

	DATE		DESCRIPTION	POST. REF.	DEBIT	CREDIT	
1							1
2							2
3							3
4							4
5							5
6							6
7							7
8							8
9							9
10							10
11							11
12							12
13							13
14							14
15							15
16							16
17							17
18							18
19							19
20							20
21							21
22							22
23							23
24							24

Name ______________________________

EXERCISE 6-22

a. Gross profit: ______________________________

b. ______________________________

____

c. ______________________________

____

d. ______________________________

____

EXERCISE 6-23

1. Advertising expense: ______________________________

2. Depreciation expense on store equipment: ______________________________

3. Insurance expense on office equipment: ______________________________

4. Interest expense on notes payable: ______________________________

5. Rent expense on office building: ______________________________

6. Salaries of office personnel: ______________________________

7. Salary of sales manager: ______________________________

8. Sales supplies used: ______________________________

EXERCISE 6-24

Sales	$463,400	**(b)** $________	$1,295,000	**(d)** $________
Cost of merchandise sold	**(a)** ________	410,000	**(c)** ________	900,000
Gross profit	83,500	277,500	275,000	600,000

EXERCISE 6-25

a.

Income Statement

b.

Name ______________________________

EXERCISE 6-26

(Optional)

Income Statement

EXERCISE 6-27

Income Statement

EXERCISE 6-28

a. Accounts Receivable: ______________________

b. Cost of Merchandise Sold: ______________________

c. Customer Refunds Payable: ______________________

d. Estimated Returns Inventory: ______________________

e. Merchandise Inventory: ______________________

f. Sales: ______________________

g. Supplies: ______________________

h. Supplies Expense: ______________________

i. Tim Button, Drawing: ______________________

j. Wages Expense: ______________________

Name ______________________________

EXERCISE 6-29

JOURNAL

PAGE

	DATE		DESCRIPTION	POST. REF.	DEBIT	CREDIT	
1			*Closing Entries*				1
2							2
3							3
4							4
5							5
6							6
7							7
8							8
9							9
10							10
11							11
12							12
13							13
14							14
15							15
16							16
17							17
18							18
19							19
20							20
21							21
22							22
23							23
24							24

EXERCISE 6-30

JOURNAL PAGE

	DATE		DESCRIPTION	POST. REF.	DEBIT	CREDIT	
1			*Closing Entries*				1
2							2
3							3
4							4
5							5
6							6
7							7
8							8
9							9
10							10
11							11
12							12
13							13
14							14
15							15
16							16
17							17
18							18
19							19
20							20
21							21
22							22
23							23
24							24

EXERCISE 6-31

a. Year 2: ______________________

Year 1: ______________________

b. ______________________

Name ______________________________

EXERCISE 6-32

a. ______________________________

b. ______________________________

APPENDIX EXERCISE 6-33

Account	Increase	Decrease	Normal Balance
Purchases	debit	**(a)** ________	**(b)** ________
Purchase Discounts	credit	**(c)** ________	credit
Purchase Returns and Allowances	**(d)** ________	**(e)** ________	**(f)** ________
Freight In	debit	**(g)** ________	debit

APPENDIX EXERCISE 6-34

JOURNAL

PAGE

DATE		DESCRIPTION	POST. REF.	DEBIT	CREDIT

APPENDIX EXERCISE 6-35

a. Purchases – (X + Y) = Net purchases

____

b. Net purchases + X = Cost of merchandise purchased

____

c. Merchandise inventory (beginning) + Cost of merchandise purchased = X

____

d. Merchandise available for sale – X = Cost of merchandise sold before estimated returns

____

e. Cost of merchandise sold before estimated returns – X = Cost of merchandise sold

____

APPENDIX EXERCISE 6-36

a.

APPENDIX EXERCISE 6-36, Concluded

b. ____

c. ____

____

APPENDIX EXERCISE 6-37

Name ______________________________

APPENDIX EXERCISE 6-38

APPENDIX EXERCISE 6-39

Name ______________________________

APPENDIX EXERCISE 6-39, Concluded

(Optional)

APPENDIX EXERCISE 6-40

JOURNAL

PAGE

	DATE		DESCRIPTION	POST. REF.	DEBIT	CREDIT	
1			*Closing Entries*				1
2							2
3							3
4							4
5							5
6							6
7							7
8							8
9							9
10							10
11							11
12							12
13							13
14							14
15							15
16							16
17							17
18							18
19							19
20							20
21							21
22							22
23							23
24							24
25							25
26							26
27							27
28							28

Name ______________________________

PROBLEM 6-1 ___

JOURNAL

PAGE

	DATE		DESCRIPTION	POST. REF.	DEBIT	CREDIT	
1							1
2							2
3							3
4							4
5							5
6							6
7							7
8							8
9							9
10							10
11							11
12							12
13							13
14							14
15							15
16							16
17							17
18							18
19							19
20							20
21							21
22							22
23							23
24							24
25							25
26							26
27							27
28							28
29							29
30							30
31							31
32							32
33							33
34							34
35							35
36							36

PROBLEM 6-1 ___, Concluded

JOURNAL

PAGE

DATE		DESCRIPTION	POST. REF.	DEBIT	CREDIT

Name ______________________________

PROBLEM 6-2 ___

JOURNAL

PAGE

DATE		DESCRIPTION	POST. REF.	DEBIT	CREDIT

PROBLEM 6-2 ___, Continued

JOURNAL

PAGE

DATE		DESCRIPTION	POST. REF.	DEBIT	CREDIT

Name ______________________________

PROBLEM 6-2 ___, Concluded

JOURNAL

PAGE

	DATE		DESCRIPTION	POST. REF.	DEBIT	CREDIT	
1							1
2							2
3							3
4							4
5							5
6							6
7							7
8							8
9							9
10							10
11							11
12							12
13							13
14							14
15							15
16							16
17							17
18							18
19							19
20							20
21							21
22							22
23							23
24							24
25							25
26							26
27							27
28							28
29							29
30							30
31							31
32							32
33							33
34							34
35							35
36							36

This Page Not Used.

Name ______________________________

PROBLEM 6-3 ___

JOURNAL

PAGE

DATE		DESCRIPTION	POST. REF.	DEBIT	CREDIT

PROBLEM 6-3 ___, Concluded

JOURNAL

PAGE

	DATE		DESCRIPTION	POST. REF.	DEBIT	CREDIT	
1							1
2							2
3							3
4							4
5							5
6							6
7							7
8							8
9							9
10							10
11							11
12							12
13							13
14							14
15							15
16							16
17							17
18							18
19							19
20							20
21							21
22							22
23							23
24							24
25							25
26							26
27							27
28							28
29							29
30							30
31							31
32							32
33							33
34							34
35							35
36							36

Name ______________________________

PROBLEM 6-4 ___

1.

JOURNAL

PAGE

	DATE		DESCRIPTION	POST. REF.	DEBIT	CREDIT	
1							1
2							2
3							3
4							4
5							5
6							6
7							7
8							8
9							9
10							10
11							11
12							12
13							13
14							14
15							15
16							16
17							17
18							18
19							19
20							20
21							21
22							22
23							23
24							24
25							25
26							26
27							27
28							28
29							29
30							30
31							31
32							32
33							33
34							34
35							35

PROBLEM 6-4 ___, Continued

JOURNAL

PAGE

	DATE		DESCRIPTION	POST. REF.	DEBIT	CREDIT	
1							1
2							2
3							3
4							4
5							5
6							6
7							7
8							8
9							9
10							10
11							11
12							12
13							13
14							14
15							15
16							16
17							17
18							18
19							19
20							20
21							21
22							22
23							23
24							24
25							25
26							26
27							27
28							28
29							29
30							30
31							31
32							32
33							33
34							34
35							35
36							36

PROBLEM 6-4 ___, Concluded

2.

JOURNAL

PAGE

	DATE		DESCRIPTION	POST. REF.	DEBIT	CREDIT	
1							1
2							2
3							3
4							4
5							5
6							6
7							7
8							8
9							9
10							10
11							11
12							12
13							13
14							14
15							15
16							16
17							17
18							18
19							19
20							20
21							21
22							22
23							23
24							24
25							25
26							26
27							27
28							28
29							29
30							30
31							31
32							32
33							33
34							34
35							35

This Page Not Used.

Name ______________________________

PROBLEM 6-5 ___

1.

Income Statement

PROBLEM 6-5 ___, Continued

2.

Statement of Owner's Equity

PROBLEM 6-5 ___, Continued

3.

Balance Sheet

PROBLEM 6-5 ___, Concluded

Balance Sheet (continued)

4. ______________________________

Name ______________________________

PROBLEM 6-6 ___

1.

Income Statement

PROBLEM 6-6 ___, Concluded

2.

JOURNAL PAGE

	DATE		DESCRIPTION	POST. REF.	DEBIT	CREDIT	
1			*Closing Entries*				1
2							2
3							3
4							4
5							5
6							6
7							7
8							8
9							9
10							10
11							11
12							12
13							13
14							14
15							15
16							16
17							17
18							18
19							19
20							20
21							21
22							22
23							23
24							24
25							25
26							26
27							27
28							28
29							29
30							30
31							31
32							32
33							33
34							34
35							35

Name ______________________________

APPENDIX PROBLEM 6-7 ___

JOURNAL

PAGE

	DATE		DESCRIPTION	POST. REF.	DEBIT	CREDIT	
1							1
2							2
3							3
4							4
5							5
6							6
7							7
8							8
9							9
10							10
11							11
12							12
13							13
14							14
15							15
16							16
17							17
18							18
19							19
20							20
21							21
22							22
23							23
24							24
25							25
26							26
27							27
28							28
29							29
30							30
31							31
32							32
33							33
34							34
35							35
36							36

APPENDIX PROBLEM 6-7 ___, Concluded

JOURNAL

PAGE

	DATE		DESCRIPTION	POST. REF.	DEBIT	CREDIT	
1							1
2							2
3							3
4							4
5							5
6							6
7							7
8							8
9							9
10							10
11							11
12							12
13							13
14							14
15							15
16							16
17							17
18							18
19							19
20							20
21							21
22							22
23							23
24							24
25							25
26							26
27							27
28							28
29							29
30							30
31							31
32							32
33							33
34							34
35							35
36							36

Name ____________________

APPENDIX PROBLEM 6-8 ___

JOURNAL

PAGE

	DATE		DESCRIPTION	POST. REF.	DEBIT	CREDIT	
1							1
2							2
3							3
4							4
5							5
6							6
7							7
8							8
9							9
10							10
11							11
12							12
13							13
14							14
15							15
16							16
17							17
18							18
19							19
20							20
21							21
22							22
23							23
24							24
25							25
26							26
27							27
28							28
29							29
30							30
31							31
32							32
33							33
34							34
35							35
36							36

APPENDIX PROBLEM 6-8 ___, Concluded

JOURNAL

PAGE

	DATE		DESCRIPTION	POST. REF.	DEBIT	CREDIT	
1							1
2							2
3							3
4							4
5							5
6							6
7							7
8							8
9							9
10							10
11							11
12							12
13							13
14							14
15							15
16							16
17							17
18							18
19							19
20							20
21							21
22							22
23							23
24							24
25							25
26							26
27							27
28							28
29							29
30							30
31							31
32							32
33							33
34							34
35							35
36							36

Name ______________________________

APPENDIX PROBLEM 6-9 ___

1. ____

____

____

____

2.

Income Statement

APPENDIX PROBLEM 6-9 ___, Continued

Income Statement (continued)

Name ______________________________

APPENDIX PROBLEM 6-9 ___, Concluded

3.

JOURNAL PAGE

	DATE		DESCRIPTION	POST. REF.	DEBIT	CREDIT	
1			*Closing Entries*				1
2							2
3							3
4							4
5							5
6							6
7							7
8							8
9							9
10							10
11							11
12							12
13							13
14							14
15							15
16							16
17							17
18							18
19							19
20							20
21							21
22							22
23							23
24							24
25							25
26							26
27							27
28							28
29							29
30							30
31							31
32							32

4. ____

This Page Not Used.

Name ______________________________

COMPREHENSIVE PROBLEM 2

1., 2., 6., and 9.

GENERAL LEDGER

ACCOUNT *Cash* ACCOUNT NO. *110*

DATE		ITEM	POST. REF.	DEBIT	CREDIT	BALANCE DEBIT	BALANCE CREDIT

ACCOUNT *Accounts Receivable* ACCOUNT NO. *112*

DATE		ITEM	POST. REF.	DEBIT	CREDIT	BALANCE DEBIT	BALANCE CREDIT

COMPREHENSIVE PROBLEM 2, Continued

ACCOUNT *Merchandise Inventory* ACCOUNT NO. *115*

DATE		ITEM	POST. REF.	DEBIT	CREDIT	BALANCE DEBIT	BALANCE CREDIT

ACCOUNT *Estimated Returns Inventory* ACCOUNT NO. *116*

DATE		ITEM	POST. REF.	DEBIT	CREDIT	BALANCE DEBIT	BALANCE CREDIT

ACCOUNT *Prepaid Insurance* ACCOUNT NO. *117*

DATE		ITEM	POST. REF.	DEBIT	CREDIT	BALANCE DEBIT	BALANCE CREDIT

Name ______________________________

COMPREHENSIVE PROBLEM 2, Continued

ACCOUNT *Store Supplies* ACCOUNT NO. *118*

DATE	ITEM	POST. REF.	DEBIT	CREDIT	BALANCE	
					DEBIT	CREDIT

ACCOUNT *Store Equipment* ACCOUNT NO. *123*

DATE	ITEM	POST. REF.	DEBIT	CREDIT	BALANCE	
					DEBIT	CREDIT

ACCOUNT *Accumulated Depreciation—Store Equipment* ACCOUNT NO. *124*

DATE	ITEM	POST. REF.	DEBIT	CREDIT	BALANCE	
					DEBIT	CREDIT

ACCOUNT *Accounts Payable* ACCOUNT NO. *210*

DATE	ITEM	POST. REF.	DEBIT	CREDIT	BALANCE	
					DEBIT	CREDIT

COMPREHENSIVE PROBLEM 2, Continued

ACCOUNT *Customer Refunds Payable* ACCOUNT NO. *211*

DATE		ITEM	POST. REF.	DEBIT	CREDIT	BALANCE	
						DEBIT	CREDIT

ACCOUNT *Salaries Payable* ACCOUNT NO. *212*

DATE		ITEM	POST. REF.	DEBIT	CREDIT	BALANCE	
						DEBIT	CREDIT

ACCOUNT *Lynn Tolley, Capital* ACCOUNT NO. *310*

DATE		ITEM	POST. REF.	DEBIT	CREDIT	BALANCE	
						DEBIT	CREDIT

ACCOUNT *Lynn Tolley, Drawing* ACCOUNT NO. *311*

DATE		ITEM	POST. REF.	DEBIT	CREDIT	BALANCE	
						DEBIT	CREDIT

Name ____________________

COMPREHENSIVE PROBLEM 2, Continued

ACCOUNT *Sales* ACCOUNT NO. *410*

DATE		ITEM	POST. REF.	DEBIT	CREDIT	BALANCE DEBIT	BALANCE CREDIT

ACCOUNT *Cost of Merchandise Sold* ACCOUNT NO. *510*

DATE		ITEM	POST. REF.	DEBIT	CREDIT	BALANCE DEBIT	BALANCE CREDIT

ACCOUNT *Sales Salaries Expense* ACCOUNT NO. *520*

DATE		ITEM	POST. REF.	DEBIT	CREDIT	BALANCE DEBIT	BALANCE CREDIT

COMPREHENSIVE PROBLEM 2, Continued

ACCOUNT *Advertising Expense* ACCOUNT NO. *521*

DATE		ITEM	POST. REF.	DEBIT	CREDIT	BALANCE	
						DEBIT	CREDIT

ACCOUNT *Depreciation Expense* ACCOUNT NO. *522*

DATE		ITEM	POST. REF.	DEBIT	CREDIT	BALANCE	
						DEBIT	CREDIT

ACCOUNT *Store Supplies Expense* ACCOUNT NO. *523*

DATE		ITEM	POST. REF.	DEBIT	CREDIT	BALANCE	
						DEBIT	CREDIT

ACCOUNT *Miscellaneous Selling Expense* ACCOUNT NO. *529*

DATE		ITEM	POST. REF.	DEBIT	CREDIT	BALANCE	
						DEBIT	CREDIT

Name ______________________________

COMPREHENSIVE PROBLEM 2, Continued

ACCOUNT *Office Salaries Expense* ACCOUNT NO. *530*

DATE		ITEM	POST. REF.	DEBIT	CREDIT	BALANCE DEBIT	BALANCE CREDIT

ACCOUNT *Rent Expense* ACCOUNT NO. *531*

DATE		ITEM	POST. REF.	DEBIT	CREDIT	BALANCE DEBIT	BALANCE CREDIT

ACCOUNT *Insurance Expense* ACCOUNT NO. *532*

DATE		ITEM	POST. REF.	DEBIT	CREDIT	BALANCE DEBIT	BALANCE CREDIT

ACCOUNT *Miscellaneous Administrative Expense* ACCOUNT NO. *539*

DATE		ITEM	POST. REF.	DEBIT	CREDIT	BALANCE DEBIT	BALANCE CREDIT

COMPREHENSIVE PROBLEM 2, Continued

1. and 2.

JOURNAL

PAGE 20

DATE		DESCRIPTION	POST. REF.	DEBIT	CREDIT

Name ______________________________

COMPREHENSIVE PROBLEM 2, Continued

JOURNAL

PAGE *20*
continued

	DATE		DESCRIPTION	POST. REF.	DEBIT	CREDIT	
1							1
2							2
3							3
4							4
5							5
6							6
7							7
8							8
9							9
10							10
11							11
12							12
13							13
14							14
15							15
16							16
17							17
18							18
19							19
20							20
21							21
22							22
23							23
24							24
25							25
26							26
27							27
28							28
29							29
30							30
31							31
32							32
33							33
34							34
35							35

COMPREHENSIVE PROBLEM 2, Continued

JOURNAL

PAGE 21

	DATE		DESCRIPTION	POST. REF.	DEBIT	CREDIT	
1							1
2							2
3							3
4							4
5							5
6							6
7							7
8							8
9							9
10							10
11							11
12							12
13							13
14							14
15							15
16							16
17							17
18							18
19							19
20							20
21							21
22							22
23							23
24							24
25							25
26							26
27							27
28							28
29							29
30							30
31							31
32							32
33							33
34							34
35							35

COMPREHENSIVE PROBLEM 2, Continued

JOURNAL

PAGE *21*
continued

DATE		DESCRIPTION	POST. REF.	DEBIT	CREDIT

COMPREHENSIVE PROBLEM 2, Continued

3.

Unadjusted Trial Balance

COMPREHENSIVE PROBLEM 2, Continued

4. and 6.

JOURNAL

PAGE 22

DATE		DESCRIPTION	POST. REF.	DEBIT	CREDIT
		Adjusting Entries			

COMPREHENSIVE PROBLEM 2, Continued

7.

Adjusted Trial Balance

Name ______________________________

COMPREHENSIVE PROBLEM 2, Continued

8.

Income Statement

COMPREHENSIVE PROBLEM 2, Continued

Statement of Owner's Equity

COMPREHENSIVE PROBLEM 2, Continued

Balance Sheet

COMPREHENSIVE PROBLEM 2, Continued

9.

JOURNAL

PAGE 23

	DATE		DESCRIPTION	POST. REF.	DEBIT	CREDIT	
1			*Closing Entries*				1
2							2
3							3
4							4
5							5
6							6
7							7
8							8
9							9
10							10
11							11
12							12
13							13
14							14
15							15
16							16
17							17
18							18
19							19
20							20
21							21
22							22
23							23
24							24
25							25
26							26
27							27
28							28
29							29
30							30
31							31
32							32
33							33
34							34
35							35

Name ______________________________

COMPREHENSIVE PROBLEM 2, Continued

10.

Post-Closing Trial Balance

Name ______________________

COMPREHENSIVE PROBLEM 2, Concluded

5. **(Optional)** *This work sheet is applicable only if the end-of-period spreadsheet (work sheet) is used.*

	A	B	C	D	E	F	G	H	I	J	K
1											
2	End-of-Period Spreadsheet (Work Sheet)										
3											
4		Unadjusted Trial Balance		Adjustments		Adjusted Trial Balance		Income Statement		Balance Sheet	
5											
6	Account Title	Dr.	Cr.	Dr.	Cr.	Dr.	Cr.	Dr.	Cr.	Dr.	Cr.
7											
8											
9											
10											
11											
12											
13											
14											
15											
16											
17											
18											
19											
20											
21											
22											
23											
24											
25											
26											
27											
28											
29											
30											
31											
32											
33											

Name ______________________________

EXERCISE 7-1

EXERCISE 7-2

a.

b.

c.

EXERCISE 7-3

a.

Portable Game Players

Date	Purchases			Cost of Merchandise Sold			Inventory		
	Quantity	Unit Cost	Total Cost	Quantity	Unit Cost	Total Cost	Quantity	Unit Cost	Total Cost

b. ____

____

____

Name ____________________

EXERCISE 7-4

Portable Game Players

Date	Purchases			Cost of Merchandise Sold			Inventory		
	Quantity	Unit Cost	Total Cost	Quantity	Unit Cost	Total Cost	Quantity	Unit Cost	Total Cost

EXERCISE 7-5

a.

Prepaid Cell Phones

Date	Purchases			Cost of Merchandise Sold			Inventory		
	Quantity	Unit Cost	Total Cost	Quantity	Unit Cost	Total Cost	Quantity	Unit Cost	Total Cost

b. ____________________

Name ____________________

EXERCISE 7-6

Prepaid Cell Phones

Date	Purchases			Cost of Merchandise Sold			Inventory		
	Quantity	Unit Cost	Total Cost	Quantity	Unit Cost	Total Cost	Quantity	Unit Cost	Total Cost

EXERCISE 7-7

a. FIFO: ____________________

____

b. LIFO: ____________________

____

Name ____________________

EXERCISE 7-8

Date	Purchases			Cost of Merchandise Sold			Inventory		
	Quantity	Unit Cost	Total Cost	Quantity	Unit Cost	Total Cost	Quantity	Unit Cost	Total Cost

EXERCISE 7-9

Date	Purchases			Cost of Merchandise Sold			Inventory		
	Quantity	Unit Cost	Total Cost	Quantity	Unit Cost	Total Cost	Quantity	Unit Cost	Total Cost

Name ______________________________

EXERCISE 7-10

Date	Purchases			Cost of Merchandise Sold			Inventory		
	Quantity	Unit Cost	Total Cost	Quantity	Unit Cost	Total Cost	Quantity	Unit Cost	Total Cost

EXERCISE 7-11

Date	Purchases			Cost of Merchandise Sold			Inventory		
	Quantity	Unit Cost	Total Cost	Quantity	Unit Cost	Total Cost	Quantity	Unit Cost	Total Cost

EXERCISE 7-12

a. First-in, first-out method: ______________________

____

b. Last-in, first-out method: ______________________

____

c. Weighted average cost method: ______________________

____

____

____

____

____

____

____

____

Name ______________________

EXERCISE 7-13

Inventory Method	Cost: Merchandise Inventory	Cost: Merchandise Sold
a. First-in, first-out		
b. Last-in, first-out		
c. Weighted average cost		

Supporting calculations:

EXERCISE 7-14

a. 1. FIFO inventory __________ LIFO inventory

2. FIFO cost of merchandise sold __________ LIFO cost of merchandise sold

3. FIFO net income __________ LIFO net income

4. FIFO income taxes __________ LIFO income taxes

b. ____

____

____

____

____

EXERCISE 7-15

	A	B	C	D	E	F	G
1				Market	Total		
2				Value			
3	Inventory Item	Inventory Quantity	Cost per Unit	per Unit (Net Realizable Value)	Cost	Market	LCM
4	Birch	100	$125	$120			
5	Cypress	75	100	108			
6	Mountain Ash	80	90	86			
7	Spruce	130	74	80			
8	Willow	60	105	98			
9	Total						

EXERCISE 7-16

____

____

____

____

____

____

____

EXERCISE 7-17

a.

Balance Sheet

Merchandise inventory	
Current assets	
Total assets	
Owner's equity	

b.

Income Statement

Cost of merchandise sold	
Gross profit	
Net income	

c.

Income Statement

Cost of merchandise sold	
Gross profit	
Net income	

d. ____________________

EXERCISE 7-18

a.

	Balance Sheet
Merchandise inventory	
Current assets	
Total assets	
Owner's equity	

b.

	Income Statement
Cost of merchandise sold	
Gross profit	
Net income	

c.

	Income Statement
Cost of merchandise sold	
Gross profit	
Net income	

d. ______________________

Name ______________________________

EXERCISE 7-19

EXERCISE 7-20

a. Apple: ______________________________

Mattel: ______________________________

b. ______________________________

EXERCISE 7-21

a. Inventory Turnover =

Kroger:

Sprouts:

Whole Foods:

b. Days' Sales in Inventory =

Kroger:

Sprouts:

Whole Foods:

c.

EXERCISE 7-21, Concluded

d.

APPENDIX EXERCISE 7-22

APPENDIX EXERCISE 7-23

APPENDIX EXERCISE 7-24

APPENDIX EXERCISE 7-25

	A	B	C
1		Cost	Retail
2			
3			
4			
5			
6			
7			
8			
9			
10			
11			
12			

APPENDIX EXERCISE 7-26

a.

	A	B	C
1			
2			
3			
4			
5			
6			
7			
8			
9			
10			
11			
12			

b. ____

____

____

____

____

Name ______________________________

APPENDIX EXERCISE 7-27

APPENDIX EXERCISE 7-28

This Page Not Used.

PROBLEM 7-1 ___

1.

Date	Purchases			Cost of Merchandise Sold			Inventory		
	Quantity	Unit Cost	Total Cost	Quantity	Unit Cost	Total Cost	Quantity	Unit Cost	Total Cost

PROBLEM 7-1 ___, Concluded

2.

JOURNAL

PAGE

	DATE		DESCRIPTION	POST. REF.	DEBIT	CREDIT	
1							1
2							2
3							3
4							4
5							5
6							6
7							7
8							8
9							9
10							10

3. ______________________________

4. ______________________________

5. ______________________________

Name ______________________

PROBLEM 7-2 ___

1.

Date	Purchases			Cost of Merchandise Sold			Inventory		
	Quantity	Unit Cost	Total Cost	Quantity	Unit Cost	Total Cost	Quantity	Unit Cost	Total Cost

Name ______________________________

PROBLEM 7-2 ___, Continued

Date	Purchases			Cost of Merchandise Sold			Inventory		
	Quantity	Unit Cost	Total Cost	Quantity	Unit Cost	Total Cost	Quantity	Unit Cost	Total Cost

PROBLEM 7-2 ___, Concluded

2.

3. ____

____

This Page Not Used.

Name ____________________

PROBLEM 7-3 ___

1.

Date	Purchases			Cost of Merchandise Sold			Inventory		
	Quantity	Unit Cost	Total Cost	Quantity	Unit Cost	Total Cost	Quantity	Unit Cost	Total Cost

PROBLEM 7-3 ___, Concluded

2.

3. ____

____

Name ___________________________

PROBLEM 7-4 ___

1., 2., and 3.

	Cost	
Inventory Method	**Merchandise Inventory**	**Merchandise Sold**
a. First-in, first-out................................	________	________
b. Last-in, first-out................................	________	________
c. Weighted average cost....................	________	________

Supporting calculations:

PROBLEM 7-4 ___, Concluded

4.

	FIFO	LIFO	Weighted Average
Sales			
Cost of merchandise sold			
Gross profit			
Inventory, __________			

Name ______________________________

PROBLEM 7-5 ___

1.

First-In, First-Out Method

Model	Quantity	Unit Cost	Total Cost

2.

Last-In, First-Out Method

Model	Quantity	Unit Cost	Total Cost

PROBLEM 7-5 ___, Concluded

3.

Weighted Average Cost Method

Model	Quantity	Unit Cost	Total Cost

Computations of unit costs:

4. a.

b.

Name ______________________________

PROBLEM 7-6 ___

	A	B	C	D	E	F	G
1	Inventory Sheet						
2	December 31						
3				Market	Total		
4				Value			
5	Inventory Item	Inventory Quantity	Cost per Unit	per Unit (Net Realizable Value)	Cost	Market	LCM
6							
7							
8							
9							
10							
11							
12							
13							
14							
15							
16							
17							
18							
19							
20							
21							
22							
23							
24							
25							
26							
27							
28							
29							
30							
31							
32							
33							
34							
35							

This Page Not Used.

Name ______________________________

APPENDIX PROBLEM 7-7 ___

1.

	A	B	C
1			
2		Cost	Retail
3			
4			
5			
6			
7			
8			
9			
10			
11			
12			
13			
14			
15			
16			
17			
18			

2.

	A	B	C
1			
2			Cost
3	a.		
4			
5			
6			
7			
8			
9			
10			
11			
12			
13			
14			
15			
16			
17	b.		
18			
19			
20			
21			
22			
23			
24			

This Page Not Used.

Name ______________________________

EXERCISE 8-1

EXERCISE 8-1, Concluded

EXERCISE 8-2

a.

Name ______________________________

EXERCISE 8-2, Concluded

b.

c.

EXERCISE 8-3

a.

b.

EXERCISE 8-3, Continued

c.

Name ______________________

EXERCISE 8-3, Concluded

d. ______________________

EXERCISE 8-4

Name ______________________________

EXERCISE 8-5

EXERCISE 8-6

Name ______________________________

EXERCISE 8-7

EXERCISE 8-8

a.

b.

EXERCISE 8-9

a.

b.

Name ____________________

EXERCISE 8-10

EXERCISE 8-11

a. ____

____

b. ____

____

EXERCISE 8-12

JOURNAL PAGE

	DATE		DESCRIPTION	POST. REF.	DEBIT	CREDIT	
1							1
2							2
3							3
4							4

EXERCISE 8-13

JOURNAL PAGE

	DATE		DESCRIPTION	POST. REF.	DEBIT	CREDIT	
1							1
2							2
3							3
4							4

Name ____________________

EXERCISE 8-14

EXERCISE 8-14, Concluded

EXERCISE 8-15

EXERCISE 8-16

a. Addition to the balance per bank: ______________________________

b. Deduction from the balance per bank: ______________________________

c. Addition to the balance per company's records: ______________________________

d. Deduction from the balance per company's records: ______________________________

EXERCISE 8-17

____

____

____

____

____

____

____

____

EXERCISE 8-18

a.

Bank Reconciliation

EXERCISE 8-18, Concluded

b. ______________________________

____

____

c. ______________________________

____

EXERCISE 8-19

JOURNAL

PAGE

	DATE		DESCRIPTION	POST. REF.	DEBIT	CREDIT	
1							1
2							2
3							3
4							4
5							5
6							6
7							7

EXERCISE 8-20

JOURNAL

PAGE

	DATE		DESCRIPTION	POST. REF.	DEBIT	CREDIT	
1							1
2							2
3							3
4							4

Name ______________________________

EXERCISE 8-21

a.

Bank Reconciliation

b. ____

EXERCISE 8-22

a. ______________________________

Name ______________________________

EXERCISE 8-22, Concluded

b.

Bank Reconciliation

EXERCISE 8-23

a. ____________________

Bank Reconciliation

Name ______________________________

EXERCISE 8-23, Concluded

b.

EXERCISE 8-24

a. and b.

JOURNAL PAGE

	DATE		DESCRIPTION	POST. REF.	DEBIT	CREDIT	
1							1
2							2
3							3
4							4
5							5
6							6
7							7
8							8
9							9
10							10
11							11
12							12

EXERCISE 8-25

EXERCISE 8-26

a.

b.

EXERCISE 8-27

a.

b.

c.

EXERCISE 8-28

a. Year 3:

Year 2:

Year 1:

b. Year 3:

Year 2:

Year 1:

Name ________________________________

EXERCISE 8-28, Concluded

c.

This Page Not Used.

Name ______________________________

PROBLEM 8-1 ___

This Page Not Used.

Name ______________________________

PROBLEM 8-2 ___

JOURNAL

PAGE

DATE		DESCRIPTION	POST. REF.	DEBIT	CREDIT

This Page Not Used.

Name ____________________

PROBLEM 8-3 ___

1.

Bank Reconciliation

PROBLEM 8-3 ___, Concluded

2.

JOURNAL PAGE

	DATE		DESCRIPTION	POST. REF.	DEBIT	CREDIT	
1							1
2							2
3							3
4							4
5							5
6							6
7							7
8							8
9							9
10							10

3. ____

____

____

____

PROBLEM 8-4 ___

1.

Bank Reconciliation

PROBLEM 8-4 ___, Concluded

2.

JOURNAL

PAGE

	DATE		DESCRIPTION	POST. REF.	DEBIT	CREDIT	
1							1
2							2
3							3
4							4
5							5
6							6
7							7
8							8
9							9
10							10
11							11
12							12

3. ____

____

____

____

Name ______________________________

PROBLEM 8-5 ___

1.

Bank Reconciliation

PROBLEM 8-5 ___, Concluded

2.

JOURNAL PAGE

	DATE		DESCRIPTION	POST. REF.	DEBIT	CREDIT	
1							1
2							2
3							3
4							4
5							5
6							6
7							7
8							8
9							9
10							10
11							11
12							12

3. ____________________

4. ____________________

Name ______________________________

EXERCISE 9-1

EXERCISE 9-2

a. MGM Resorts International: ______________________________

b. Johnson & Johnson: ______________________________

c. ______________________________

EXERCISE 9-3

JOURNAL

PAGE

DATE		DESCRIPTION	POST. REF.	DEBIT	CREDIT

Name ______________________________

EXERCISE 9-4

JOURNAL PAGE

	DATE		DESCRIPTION	POST. REF.	DEBIT	CREDIT	
1							1
2							2
3							3
4							4
5							5
6							6
7							7
8							8
9							9
10							10
11							11
12							12
13							13
14							14
15							15
16							16
17							17
18							18
19							19
20							20
21							21
22							22

EXERCISE 9-5

a. and b.

JOURNAL PAGE

	DATE		DESCRIPTION	POST. REF.	DEBIT	CREDIT	
1							1
2							2
3							3
4							4
5							5
6							6
7							7
8							8

EXERCISE 9-6

a. ______________________

b. ______________________

c. ______________________

d. ______________________

EXERCISE 9-7

Account	**Due Date**	**Number of Days Past Due**
Avalanche Auto	August 8	
Bales Auto	October 11	
Derby Auto Repair	June 23	
Lucky's Auto Repair	September 2	
Pit Stop Auto	September 19	
Reliable Auto Repair	July 15	
Trident Auto	August 24	
Valley Repair & Tow	May 17	

EXERCISE 9-8

a.

Customer	**Due Date**	**Number of Days Past Due**
Conover Industries	March 22	
Keystone Company	July 1	
Moxie Creek Inc.	July 25	
Rainbow Company	September 10	
Swanson Company	August 3	

EXERCISE 9-8, Concluded

b.

	A	B	C	D	E	F	G
1	Aging of Receivables Schedule						
2	August 31						
3			Not Past	Days Past Due			
4	Customer	Balance	Due	1–30	31–60	61–90	Over 90
5	Academy Industries Inc.	3,000	3,000				
6	Ascent Company	4,500		4,500			
21	Zoot Company	5,000			5,000		
22	Subtotals	1,050,000	600,000	220,000	115,000	85,000	30,000
23							
24							
25							
26							
27							
28							
29							
30							

EXERCISE 9-9

	BALANCE	NOT PAST DUE	DAYS PAST DUE			
			1–30	31–60	61–90	OVER 90

EXERCISE 9-10

JOURNAL PAGE

	DATE		DESCRIPTION	POST. REF.	DEBIT	CREDIT	
1							1
2							2
3							3
4							4
5							5
6							6
7							7

EXERCISE 9-11

Age Interval	Balance	Estimated Uncollectible Accounts Percent	Estimated Uncollectible Accounts Amount
Not past due	$3,250,000	0.8%	$
1–30 days past due	1,050,000	2.4	
31–60 days past due	780,000	7.0	
61–90 days past due	320,000	18.0	
91–180 days past due	240,000	34.0	
Over 180 days past due	150,000	85.0	
Total	$5,790,000		$

EXERCISE 9-12

JOURNAL PAGE

	DATE		DESCRIPTION	POST. REF.	DEBIT	CREDIT	
1							1
2							2
3							3
4							4
5							5
6							6
7							7

EXERCISE 9-13

a.

JOURNAL PAGE

	DATE		DESCRIPTION	POST. REF.	DEBIT	CREDIT	
1							1
2							2
3							3
4							4
5							5
6							6
7							7
8							8
9							9
10							10
11							11
12							12
13							13
14							14
15							15
16							16
17							17
18							18
19							19
20							20
21							21
22							22
23							23
24							24
25							25
26							26
27							27
28							28
29							29
30							30
31							31
32							32

EXERCISE 9-13, Continued

b.

JOURNAL

PAGE

DATE		DESCRIPTION	POST. REF.	DEBIT	CREDIT

Name ______________________________

EXERCISE 9-13, Concluded

JOURNAL

PAGE

	DATE		DESCRIPTION	POST. REF.	DEBIT	CREDIT	
1							1
2							2
3							3
4							4
5							5
6							6
7							7
8							8
9							9
10							10

c.

EXERCISE 9-14

a.

JOURNAL

PAGE

	DATE		DESCRIPTION	POST. REF.	DEBIT	CREDIT	
1							1
2							2
3							3
4							4
5							5
6							6
7							7
8							8
9							9
10							10
11							11
12							12
13							13
14							14
15							15
16							16
17							17
18							18
19							19
20							20
21							21
22							22
23							23
24							24
25							25
26							26
27							27
28							28
29							29
30							30
31							31
32							32

Name ______________________________

EXERCISE 9-14, Continued

b.

JOURNAL

PAGE

DATE		DESCRIPTION	POST. REF.	DEBIT	CREDIT

EXERCISE 9-14, Concluded

JOURNAL

PAGE

	DATE		DESCRIPTION	POST. REF.	DEBIT	CREDIT	
1							1
2							2
3							3
4							4
5							5
6							6
7							7
8							8
9							9
10							10

Computations:

Aging Class (Number of Days Past Due)	**Receivables Balance on December 31**	**Estimated Doubtful Accounts Percent**	**Estimated Doubtful Accounts Amount**
0–30 days	$320,000	1%	$
31–60 days	110,000	3	
61–90 days	24,000	10	
91–120 days	18,000	33	
More than 120 days	43,000	75	
Total receivables	$515,000		
			$

c.

EXERCISE 9-15

EXERCISE 9-16

a. ____________________

b. ____________________

Allowance for Doubtful Accounts

EXERCISE 9-17

a.

JOURNAL PAGE

	DATE		DESCRIPTION	POST. REF.	DEBIT	CREDIT	
1							1
2							2
3							3
4							4
5							5
6							6
7							7
8							8
9							9
10							10

b.

JOURNAL PAGE

	DATE		DESCRIPTION	POST. REF.	DEBIT	CREDIT	
1							1
2							2
3							3
4							4
5							5
6							6
7							7
8							8
9							9
10							10
11							11
12							12
13							13
14							14
15							15
16							16
17							17
18							18
19							19
20							20

Name ______________________________

EXERCISE 9-17, Concluded

c. ______________________________

EXERCISE 9-18

a.

JOURNAL PAGE

	DATE		DESCRIPTION	POST. REF.	DEBIT	CREDIT	
1							1
2							2
3							3
4							4
5							5
6							6
7							7
8							8
9							9
10							10

EXERCISE 9-18, Concluded

b.

JOURNAL

PAGE

	DATE		DESCRIPTION	POST. REF.	DEBIT	CREDIT	
1							1
2							2
3							3
4							4
5							5
6							6
7							7
8							8
9							9
10							10
11							11
12							12
13							13
14							14
15							15
16							16
17							17
18							18
19							19
20							20

Computations:

Aging Class (Number of Days Past Due)	**Receivables Balance on December 31**	**Estimated Doubtful Accounts Percent**	**Estimated Doubtful Accounts Amount**
0–30 days	$ 715,000	1%	$
31–60 days	310,000	2	
61–90 days	102,000	15	
91–120 days	76,000	30	
More than 120 days	97,000	60	
Total receivables	$1,300,000		
			$

Name ______________________

EXERCISE 9-18, Concluded

c. ______________________

EXERCISE 9-19

	Date of Note	Face Amount	Interest Rate	Term of Note	Due Date	Interest Due
a.	January 10	$40,000	5%	90 days	______	$______
b.	March 19	18,000	8	180 days	______	______
c.	June 5	90,000	7	30 days	______	______
d.	September 8	36,000	3	90 days	______	______
e.	November 20	27,000	4	60 days	______	______

EXERCISE 9-20

a. ______________________

b. ______________________

c.

JOURNAL PAGE

	DATE		DESCRIPTION	POST. REF.	DEBIT	CREDIT	
1							1
2							2
3							3
4							4
5							5
6							6
7							7
8							8

EXERCISE 9-21

a. ______________________

b. ______________________

c. ______________________

d. ______________________

____

e. ______________________

____

EXERCISE 9-22

JOURNAL

PAGE

DATE		DESCRIPTION	POST. REF.	DEBIT	CREDIT

Name ______________________________

EXERCISE 9-23

JOURNAL PAGE

	DATE		DESCRIPTION	POST. REF.	DEBIT	CREDIT	
1							1
2							2
3							3
4							4
5							5
6							6
7							7
8							8
9							9
10							10
11							11
12							12
13							13
14							14
15							15
16							16
17							17

EXERCISE 9-24

JOURNAL

PAGE

	DATE		DESCRIPTION	POST. REF.	DEBIT	CREDIT	
1							1
2							2
3							3
4							4
5							5
6							6
7							7
8							8
9							9
10							10
11							11
12							12
13							13
14							14
15							15
16							16
17							17
18							18
19							19
20							20
21							21
22							22
23							23
24							24
25							25
26							26
27							27
28							28
29							29
30							30
31							31
32							32

Name ______________________________

EXERCISE 9-25

(Optional)

Balance Sheet

EXERCISE 9-26

a. and b.

	Year 2	**Year 1**
Sales	$7,620,000	$7,450,000
Accounts receivable	857,000	800,000
Average accounts receivable		
Accounts receivable turnover		
Average daily sales		
Days' sales in receivables		

c.

Name ____________________

EXERCISE 9-27

a. and b.

	Year 2	**Year 1**
Sales	$8,082	$8,268
Accounts receivable	647	670
Average accounts receivable	________	________
Accounts receivable turnover	________	________
Average daily sales	________	________
Days' sales in receivables	________	________

c. ____________________

EXERCISE 9-28

a. and b.

	Year 2	Year 1
Sales	$3,522	$3,283
Accounts receivable	81	68
Average accounts receivable	________	________
Accounts receivable turnover	________	________
Average daily sales	________	________
Days' sales in receivables	________	________

c.

Name ______________________________

EXERCISE 9-29

a. Campbell Soup: ______________________________

American Eagle Outfitters: ______________________________

b. ______________________________

c. ______________________________

This Page Not Used.

PROBLEM 9-1 ___

1. and 2.

Allowance for Doubtful Accounts

Bad Debt Expense

3. ______________________

4. a. ______________________

b. ______________________

c. ______________________

PROBLEM 9-1 ___, Continued

2.

JOURNAL

PAGE

DATE		DESCRIPTION	POST. REF.	DEBIT	CREDIT

Name ______________________________

PROBLEM 9-1 ___, Concluded

JOURNAL

PAGE

DATE		DESCRIPTION	POST. REF.	DEBIT	CREDIT

This Page Not Used.

Name ______________________

PROBLEM 9-2 ___

1.

Customer	Due Date	Number of Days Past Due

4.

JOURNAL PAGE

	DATE		DESCRIPTION	POST. REF.	DEBIT	CREDIT	
1							1
2							2
3							3
4							4
5							5
6							6
7							7

5. ______________________

PROBLEM 9-2 ___, Concluded

2. and 3.

	A	B	C	D	E	F	G	H
1	Aging of Receivables Schedule							
2	December 31, 20Y__							
3			Not Past	Days Past Due				
4	Customer	Balance	Due	1–30	31–60	61–90	91–120	Over 120
5								
6								
30								
31	Subtotals							
32								
33								
34								
35								
36								
37								
38								
39								
40								
41								
42								
43								
44								
45								
46								

Name ______________________________

PROBLEM 9-3 ___

1.

Year	Bad Debt Expense			Balance of Allowance Account, End of Year
	Expense Actually Reported	Expense Based on Estimate	Increase (Decrease) in Amount of Expense	

2. ______________________________

This Page Not Used.

Name ______________________________

PROBLEM 9-4 ___

1.

Note	(a) Due Date	(b) Interest Due at Maturity
1.		
2.		
3.		
4.		
5.		
6.		

PROBLEM 9-4 ___, Concluded

2., 3., and 4.

JOURNAL

PAGE

	DATE		DESCRIPTION	POST. REF.	DEBIT	CREDIT	
1							1
2							2
3							3
4							4
5							5
6							6
7							7
8							8
9							9
10							10
11							11
12							12
13							13
14							14
15							15
16							16
17							17
18							18
19							19
20							20
21							21
22							22
23							23
24							24
25							25
26							26
27							27
28							28

Name ______________________________

PROBLEM 9-5 ___

JOURNAL

PAGE

DATE		DESCRIPTION	POST. REF.	DEBIT	CREDIT

This Page Not Used.

Name ______________________________

PROBLEM 9-6 ___

JOURNAL

PAGE

DATE		DESCRIPTION	POST. REF.	DEBIT	CREDIT

PROBLEM 9-6 ___, Concluded

JOURNAL

PAGE

DATE		DESCRIPTION	POST. REF.	DEBIT	CREDIT

Name ______________________________

EXERCISE 10-1

a. New printing press costs debited to the asset account: ______________________________

b. Used printing press costs debited to the asset account: ______________________________

EXERCISE 10-2

a. ______________________________

b. ______________________________

EXERCISE 10-3

EXERCISE 10-4

a. ____________________

b. ____________________

EXERCISE 10-5

a. 10 years: ____________________

b. 8 years: ____________________

c. 25 years: ____________________

d. 40 years: ____________________

e. 5 years: ____________________

f. 4 years: ____________________

g. 20 years: ____________________

EXERCISE 10-6

____

EXERCISE 10-7

____

Name ______________________________

EXERCISE 10-8

a.

Truck No.	Rate per Mile	Miles Operated	Credit to Accumulated Depreciation
1	______	______	$______
2	______	______	$______
3	______	______	$______
4	______	______	$______
Total			$______

b.

JOURNAL PAGE

	DATE		DESCRIPTION	POST. REF.	DEBIT	CREDIT	
1							1
2							2
3							3
4							4
5							5

EXERCISE 10-9

a. Straight-line method:

First year: ______________________________

Second year: ______________________________

b. Double-declining-balance method:

First year: ______________________________

Second year: ______________________________

EXERCISE 10-10

a. Straight-line method:

____

b. Double-declining-balance method:

Year 1: ______________________________

Year 2: ______________________________

EXERCISE 10-11

a. Straight-line method:

Year 1: ______________________

Year 2: ______________________

b. Double-declining-balance method:

Year 1: ______________________

Year 2: ______________________

EXERCISE 10-12

a. ______________________

b. ______________________

c. ______________________

EXERCISE 10-13

1. ______________________
2. ______________________
3. ______________________
4. ______________________
5. ______________________
6. ______________________
7. ______________________
8. ______________________
9. ______________________
10. ______________________

EXERCISE 10-14

1. ______________________
2. ______________________
3. ______________________
4. ______________________
5. ______________________
6. ______________________
7. ______________________
8. ______________________
9. ______________________
10. ______________________

Name ____________________

EXERCISE 10-15

JOURNAL PAGE

	DATE		DESCRIPTION	POST. REF.	DEBIT	CREDIT	
1							1
2							2
3							3
4							4
5							5
6							6
7							7
8							8
9							9
10							10
11							11
12							12

EXERCISE 10-16

a. and b.

JOURNAL PAGE

	DATE		DESCRIPTION	POST. REF.	DEBIT	CREDIT	
1							1
2							2
3							3
4							4
5							5
6							6
7							7
8							8
9							9
10							10

EXERCISE 10-17

a.

b.

JOURNAL PAGE

	DATE		DESCRIPTION	POST. REF.	DEBIT	CREDIT	
1							1
2							2
3							3
4							4
5							5
6							6
7							7
8							8
9							9
10							10
11							11
12							12
13							13
14							14
15							15

EXERCISE 10-18

a. Year 1: ______________________

Year 2: ______________________

Year 3: ______________________

b. ______________________

Name ______________________________

EXERCISE 10-18, Concluded

c. and d.

JOURNAL PAGE

	DATE		DESCRIPTION	POST. REF.	DEBIT	CREDIT	
1							1
2							2
3							3
4							4
5							5
6							6
7							7
8							8
9							9
10							10
11							11
12							12
13							13
14							14
15							15

EXERCISE 10-19

a. ______________________________

____

b.

JOURNAL PAGE

	DATE		DESCRIPTION	POST. REF.	DEBIT	CREDIT	
1							1
2							2
3							3
4							4
5							5

EXERCISE 10-20

a. ______________________

____

b.

JOURNAL PAGE

	DATE		DESCRIPTION	POST. REF.	DEBIT	CREDIT	
1							1
2							2
3							3
4							4
5							5

EXERCISE 10-21

a.

	CURRENT YEAR	PRECEDING YEAR

EXERCISE 10-21, Concluded

b.

EXERCISE 10-22

EXERCISE 10-23

a. Fixed Asset Turnover Ratio =

Amazon:

Netflix:

b.

c.

Name ____________________

EXERCISE 10-24

a. Fixed Asset Turnover Ratio =

Verizon:

b.

EXERCISE 10-25

a. Fixed Asset Turnover Ratio =

FedEx:

UPS:

b.

c.

Name ______________________________

EXERCISE 10-26

a. Fixed Asset Turnover Ratio =

Alphabet (Google) Inc.:

Comcast:

Wal-Mart:

b.

APPENDIX EXERCISE 10-27

a.

b.

APPENDIX EXERCISE 10-28

a.

b.

Name ______________________________

APPENDIX EXERCISE 10-29

a. and b.

JOURNAL

PAGE

	DATE		DESCRIPTION	POST. REF.	DEBIT	CREDIT	
1							1
2							2
3							3
4							4
5							5
6							6
7							7
8							8
9							9
10							10
11							11
12							12
13							13
14							14
15							15

APPENDIX EXERCISE 10-30

a. and b.

JOURNAL

PAGE

	DATE		DESCRIPTION	POST. REF.	DEBIT	CREDIT	
1							1
2							2
3							3
4							4
5							5
6							6
7							7
8							8
9							9
10							10
11							11
12							12
13							13
14							14
15							15

Name ______________________________

PROBLEM 10-1 ___

1. and 2.

Item	Land	Land Improvements	Building	Other Accounts
a.				
b.				
c.				
d.				
e.				
f.				
g.				
h.				
i.				
j.				
k.				
l.				
m.				
n.				
o.				
p.				
q.				
r.				
s.				
Total				

PROBLEM 10-1 ___, Concluded

3. ______________________________

4. ______________________________

Name ______________________

PROBLEM 10-2 ___

1.

	Depreciation Expense		
Year	**a. Straight-Line Method**	**b. Units-of-Activity Method**	**c. Double-Declining-Balance Method**
______	______	______	______
______	______	______	______
______	______	______	______
______	______	______	______
Total	______	______	______

Supporting Calculations:

2. ______________________

3. ______________________

This Page Not Used.

Name ______________________________

PROBLEM 10-3 ___

a.

Straight-Line Method

Year	Calculations	Depreciation Expense
1		
2		
3		
4		

b.

Units-of-Activity Method

Year	Calculations	Depreciation Expense
1		
2		
3		
4		

c.

Double-Declining-Balance Method

Year	Calculations	Depreciation Expense
1		
2		
3		
4		

This Page Not Used.

Name ______________________________

PROBLEM 10-4 ___

1. a.

Straight-Line Method

Year	Depreciation Expense	Accumulated Depreciation, End of Year	Book Value, End of Year
1			
2			
3			
4			
5			

b.

Double-Declining-Balance Method

Year	Depreciation Expense	Accumulated Depreciation, End of Year	Book Value, End of Year
1			
2			
3			
4			
5			

PROBLEM 10-4 ___, Concluded

2.

JOURNAL PAGE

	DATE		DESCRIPTION	POST. REF.	DEBIT	CREDIT	
1							1
2							2
3							3
4							4
5							5
6							6
7							7
8							8

3.

JOURNAL PAGE

	DATE		DESCRIPTION	POST. REF.	DEBIT	CREDIT	
1							1
2							2
3							3
4							4
5							5
6							6
7							7
8							8

Name ______________________________

PROBLEM 10-5 ___

JOURNAL

PAGE

DATE		DESCRIPTION	POST. REF.	DEBIT	CREDIT

PROBLEM 10-5 ___, Concluded

JOURNAL

PAGE

DATE		DESCRIPTION	POST. REF.	DEBIT	CREDIT

Name ______________________________

PROBLEM 10-6 ___

1. a. ____

____

____

b. ____

____

____

c. ____

____

____

2.

JOURNAL

PAGE

	DATE		DESCRIPTION	POST. REF.	DEBIT	CREDIT	
1							1
2							2
3							3
4							4
5							5
6							6
7							7
8							8
9							9
10							10
11							11
12							12
13							13
14							14
15							15

This Page Not Used.

Name ______________________________

EXERCISE 11-1

EXERCISE 11-2

a. and b.

JOURNAL PAGE

	DATE		DESCRIPTION	POST. REF.	DEBIT	CREDIT	
1							1
2							2
3							3
4							4
5							5
6							6
7							7
8							8
9							9
10							10
11							11
12							12
13							13
14							14
15							15

EXERCISE 11-3

a. and b.

JOURNAL

PAGE

	DATE		DESCRIPTION	POST. REF.	DEBIT	CREDIT	
1							1
2							2
3							3
4							4
5							5
6							6
7							7
8							8
9							9
10							10
11							11
12							12
13							13
14							14
15							15

EXERCISE 11-4

a. ______________________

b. (1) ______________________

(2) ______________________

c. ______________________

EXERCISE 11-5

a. and b.

JOURNAL PAGE

	DATE		DESCRIPTION	POST. REF.	DEBIT	CREDIT	
1							1
2							2
3							3
4							4
5							5
6							6
7							7
8							8

EXERCISE 11-6

a. and b.

JOURNAL PAGE

	DATE		DESCRIPTION	POST. REF.	DEBIT	CREDIT	
1							1
2							2
3							3
4							4
5							5
6							6
7							7
8							8

EXERCISE 11-7

a. and b.

JOURNAL PAGE

	DATE		DESCRIPTION	POST. REF.	DEBIT	CREDIT	
1							1
2							2
3							3
4							4
5							5
6							6
7							7
8							8
9							9
10							10
11							11
12							12
13							13
14							14
15							15
16							16

Name ______________________________

EXERCISE 11-8

a. ______________________________

____

b. ______________________________

____

c. ______________________________

____

EXERCISE 11-9

a.

b.

EXERCISE 11-10

	Consultant	Computer Programmer	Administrator
Regular earnings	$	$	$
Overtime earnings			
Gross pay	$	$	$
Less: Social security tax	$	$	$
Medicare tax			
Federal income tax withheld			
	$	$	$
Net pay	$	$	$

EXERCISE 11-10, Concluded

Withholding Supporting Calculations:

	CONSULTANT	COMPUTER PROGRAMMER	ADMINISTRATOR

EXERCISE 11-11

a. ____

EXERCISE 11-11, Concluded

b. and c.

JOURNAL

PAGE

	DATE		DESCRIPTION	POST. REF.	DEBIT	CREDIT	
1							1
2							2
3							3
4							4
5							5
6							6
7							7
8							8
9							9
10							10
11							11
12							12
13							13
14							14
15							15
16							16
17							17
18							18

EXERCISE 11-12

a.

EXERCISE 11-12, Concluded

b.

JOURNAL

PAGE

DATE		DESCRIPTION	POST. REF.	DEBIT	CREDIT

EXERCISE 11-13

a. and b.

JOURNAL

PAGE

DATE		DESCRIPTION	POST. REF.	DEBIT	CREDIT

EXERCISE 11-14

a. and b.

JOURNAL PAGE

	DATE		DESCRIPTION	POST. REF.	DEBIT	CREDIT	
1							1
2							2
3							3
4							4
5							5
6							6
7							7
8							8
9							9
10							10
11							11
12							12
13							13
14							14
15							15
16							16
17							17
18							18
19							19
20							20
21							21
22							22

EXERCISE 11-15

EXERCISE 11-16

a. ______________________________

b. ______________________________

c. ______________________________

d. ______________________________

e. ______________________________

Name ______________________________

EXERCISE 11-17

a.

JOURNAL PAGE

	DATE		DESCRIPTION	POST. REF.	DEBIT	CREDIT	
1							1
2							2
3							3
4							4
5							5

b. ______________________________

____

____

____

____

____

____

EXERCISE 11-18

a.

JOURNAL PAGE

	DATE		DESCRIPTION	POST. REF.	DEBIT	CREDIT	
1							1
2							2
3							3
4							4
5							5
6							6
7							7
8							8
9							9

EXERCISE 11-18, Concluded

b.

EXERCISE 11-19

Name ________________________________

EXERCISE 11-20

a. and b.

JOURNAL PAGE

	DATE		DESCRIPTION	POST. REF.	DEBIT	CREDIT	
1							1
2							2
3							3
4							4
5							5
6							6
7							7
8							8
9							9
10							10

EXERCISE 11-21

a. ________________________________

b.

JOURNAL PAGE

	DATE		DESCRIPTION	POST. REF.	DEBIT	CREDIT	
1							1
2							2
3							3
4							4
5							5
6							6

EXERCISE 11-21, Concluded

c. ______________________

EXERCISE 11-22

a.

JOURNAL PAGE

	DATE		DESCRIPTION	POST. REF.	DEBIT	CREDIT	
1							1
2							2
3							3
4							4
5							5

b. ______________________

Name ______________________________

EXERCISE 11-23

a. Quick Ratio =

Previous year:

Current year:

b.

EXERCISE 11-24

a.

	Apple Inc:	HP, Inc.:
Quick Ratio:	________	________

Computations:

b.

Name ______________________________

PROBLEM 11-1 ___

1.

JOURNAL

PAGE ______

DATE		DESCRIPTION	POST. REF.	DEBIT	CREDIT

PROBLEM 11-1 ___, Concluded

JOURNAL

PAGE

	DATE		DESCRIPTION	POST. REF.	DEBIT	CREDIT	
1							1
2							2
3							3
4							4
5							5
6							6
7							7
8							8
9							9
10							10
11							11
12							12
13							13
14							14
15							15
16							16
17							17
18							18

2.

JOURNAL

PAGE

	DATE		DESCRIPTION	POST. REF.	DEBIT	CREDIT	
1							1
2							2
3							3
4							4
5							5
6							6
7							7
8							8
9							9
10							10
11							11
12							12
13							13
14							14

PROBLEM 11-2 ___

1.

JOURNAL PAGE

	DATE		DESCRIPTION	POST. REF.	DEBIT	CREDIT	
1							1
2							2
3							3
4							4
5							5
6							6
7							7
8							8
9							9
10							10
11							11
12							12
13							13
14							14
15							15
16							16
17							17
18							18
19							19
20							20
21							21
22							22
23							23
24							24
25							25
26							26
27							27
28							28
29							29
30							30
31							31
32							32
33							33
34							34
35							35

PROBLEM 11-2 ___, Concluded

2.

JOURNAL

PAGE

	DATE		DESCRIPTION	POST. REF.	DEBIT	CREDIT	
1							1
2							2
3							3
4							4
5							5
6							6
7							7
8							8
9							9
10							10
11							11
12							12
13							13
14							14
15							15
16							16
17							17
18							18
19							19
20							20
21							21
22							22
23							23
24							24
25							25
26							26
27							27
28							28
29							29
30							30
31							31
32							32
33							33
34							34
35							35

Name ______________________________

PROBLEM 11-3 ___

1.

Employee	Gross Earnings	Federal Income Tax Withheld	Social Security Tax Withheld	Medicare Tax Withheld

PROBLEM 11-3 ___, Concluded

2. Payroll taxes incurred and paid by employer:

   a. Social security tax paid by employer .... $ ____________

   b. Medicare tax paid by employer .... ____________

   c. State unemployment compensation tax .... ____________

   Calculations and comments:

   ____

   ____

   ____

   ____

   ____

   ____

   ____

   ____

   d. Federal unemployment compensation tax .... ____________

   e. Total payroll tax expense .... $ ____________

PROBLEM 11-4 ___

1.

PAYROLL FOR WEEK ENDING *December 9, 20Y8*

	EMPLOYEE	TOTAL HOURS	EARNINGS			DEDUCTIONS					PAID		ACCOUNTS DEBITED		
			REGULAR	OVERTIME	TOTAL	SOCIAL SECURITY TAX	MEDICARE TAX	FEDERAL INCOME TAX	RETIREMENT SAVINGS	TOTAL	NET PAY	CK. NO.	SALES SALARIES EXPENSE	OFFICE SALARIES EXPENSE	
1															1
2															2
3															3
4															4
5															5
6															6
7															7
8															8
9															9
10															10
11															11
12															12

PROBLEM 11-4 ___, Concluded

2.

JOURNAL PAGE

	DATE		DESCRIPTION	POST. REF.	DEBIT	CREDIT	
1							1
2							2
3							3
4							4
5							5
6							6
7							7
8							8
9							9
10							10
11							11
12							12

Name ______________________________

PROBLEM 11-5 ___

1.

JOURNAL

PAGE

	DATE		DESCRIPTION	POST. REF.	DEBIT	CREDIT	
1							1
2							2
3							3
4							4
5							5
6							6
7							7
8							8
9							9
10							10
11							11
12							12
13							13
14							14
15							15
16							16
17							17
18							18
19							19
20							20
21							21
22							22
23							23
24							24
25							25
26							26
27							27
28							28
29							29
30							30
31							31
32							32
33							33
34							34
35							35

PROBLEM 11-5 ___, Continued

JOURNAL

PAGE

	DATE		DESCRIPTION	POST. REF.	DEBIT	CREDIT	
1							1
2							2
3							3
4							4
5							5
6							6
7							7
8							8
9							9
10							10
11							11
12							12
13							13
14							14
15							15
16							16
17							17
18							18
19							19
20							20
21							21
22							22
23							23
24							24
25							25
26							26
27							27
28							28
29							29
30							30
31							31
32							32
33							33
34							34
35							35
36							36

Name ______________________________

PROBLEM 11-5 ___, Continued

JOURNAL

PAGE

DATE		DESCRIPTION	POST. REF.	DEBIT	CREDIT

PROBLEM 11-5 ___, Concluded

2.

JOURNAL

PAGE

	DATE		DESCRIPTION	POST. REF.	DEBIT	CREDIT	
1							1
2							2
3							3
4							4
5							5
6							6
7							7
8							8
9							9
10							10
11							11
12							12
13							13
14							14
15							15
16							16
17							17
18							18

Name ______________________________

COMPREHENSIVE PROBLEM 3

1.

JOURNAL

PAGE

DATE		DESCRIPTION	POST. REF.	DEBIT	CREDIT

COMPREHENSIVE PROBLEM 3, Continued

JOURNAL

PAGE

DATE		DESCRIPTION	POST. REF.	DEBIT	CREDIT

Name ______________________________

COMPREHENSIVE PROBLEM 3, Continued

JOURNAL

PAGE

	DATE		DESCRIPTION	POST. REF.	DEBIT	CREDIT	
1							1
2							2
3							3
4							4
5							5
6							6
7							7
8							8
9							9
10							10
11							11
12							12
13							13
14							14
15							15
16							16
17							17
18							18
19							19
20							20
21							21
22							22
23							23
24							24
25							25
26							26
27							27
28							28
29							29
30							30
31							31
32							32
33							33
34							34
35							35
36							36

COMPREHENSIVE PROBLEM 3, Continued

2.

Bank Reconciliation

3.

JOURNAL PAGE

	DATE		DESCRIPTION	POST. REF.	DEBIT	CREDIT	
1							1
2							2
3							3
4							4
5							5

COMPREHENSIVE PROBLEM 3, Continued

4.

JOURNAL

PAGE

	DATE		DESCRIPTION	POST. REF.	DEBIT	CREDIT	
1							1
2							2
3							3
4							4
5							5
6							6
7							7
8							8
9							9
10							10
11							11
12							12
13							13
14							14
15							15
16							16
17							17
18							18
19							19
20							20
21							21
22							22
23							23
24							24
25							25
26							26
27							27
28							28
29							29
30							30
31							31
32							32
33							33
34							34
35							35

COMPREHENSIVE PROBLEM 3, Continued

JOURNAL

PAGE

DATE		DESCRIPTION	POST. REF.	DEBIT	CREDIT

Name ______________________________

COMPREHENSIVE PROBLEM 3, Continued

5.

Balance Sheet

COMPREHENSIVE PROBLEM 3, Concluded

Balance Sheet

Name ______________________________

EXERCISE 12-1

JOURNAL PAGE

	DATE		DESCRIPTION	POST. REF.	DEBIT	CREDIT	
1							1
2							2
3							3
4							4
5							5
6							6
7							7
8							8
9							9

EXERCISE 12-2

JOURNAL PAGE

	DATE		DESCRIPTION	POST. REF.	DEBIT	CREDIT	
1							1
2							2
3							3
4							4
5							5
6							6
7							7
8							8
9							9
10							10

EXERCISE 12-3

	Hawes	Albright
a.	______	______
b.	______	______
c.	______	______
d.	______	______
e.	______	______

Details:

	Hawes	Albright	Total
a.			
b.			
c.			
d.			
e.			

Name ____________________

EXERCISE 12-4

	Hawes	Albright
a.	____________	____________
b.	____________	____________
c.	____________	____________
d.	____________	____________
e.	____________	____________

Details:

	Hawes	Albright	Total
a.			
b.			
c.			
d.			
e.			

EXERCISE 12-5

	Leigh Meadows	Byron Leef	Total

EXERCISE 12-6

a. ______________________

b. ______________________

Name ______________________________

EXERCISE 12-7

a.

	Farley	Clark	Total

____

____

b.

JOURNAL PAGE

	DATE		DESCRIPTION	POST. REF.	DEBIT	CREDIT	
1							1
2							2
3							3
4							4
5							5
6							6
7							7
8							8
9							9
10							10
11							11
12							12
13							13
14							14
15							15

EXERCISE 12-7, Concluded

c. ______________________

EXERCISE 12-8

a.

	WLKT Partners	Madison Sanders	Observer Newspaper, LLC	Total

Name ______________________________

EXERCISE 12-8, Continued

b.

JOURNAL

PAGE

	DATE		DESCRIPTION	POST. REF.	DEBIT	CREDIT	
1							1
2							2
3							3
4							4
5							5
6							6
7							7
8							8
9							9
10							10
11							11
12							12
13							13
14							14
15							15
16							16
17							17
18							18
19							19
20							20
21							21
22							22
23							23
24							24
25							25
26							26
27							27
28							28

EXERCISE 12-8, Concluded

c.

Statement of Members' Equity

	WLKT PARTNERS	MADISON SANDERS	OBSERVER NEWSPAPER, LLC	TOTAL LLC CAPITAL

d.

Name ______________________________

EXERCISE 12-9

a. and b.

JOURNAL PAGE

	DATE		DESCRIPTION	POST. REF.	DEBIT	CREDIT	
1							1
2							2
3							3
4							4
5							5

EXERCISE 12-10

a.

JOURNAL PAGE

	DATE		DESCRIPTION	POST. REF.	DEBIT	CREDIT	
1							1
2							2
3							3
4							4
5							5
6							6
7							7
8							8
9							9
10							10

b.

EXERCISE 12-11

a.

JOURNAL PAGE

	DATE		DESCRIPTION	POST. REF.	DEBIT	CREDIT	
1							1
2							2
3							3
4							4
5							5
6							6
7							7

b.

c. ______________________________

Name ______________________________

EXERCISE 12-12

a.

b.

JOURNAL

PAGE

	DATE		DESCRIPTION	POST. REF.	DEBIT	CREDIT	
1							1
2							2
3							3
4							4
5							5
6							6
7							7

EXERCISE 12-12, Concluded

c.

EXERCISE 12-13

a.

JOURNAL PAGE

	DATE		DESCRIPTION	POST. REF.	DEBIT	CREDIT	
1							1
2							2
3							3
4							4
5							5
6							6
7							7

EXERCISE 12-13, Continued

b. (1)

JOURNAL PAGE

	DATE		DESCRIPTION	POST. REF.	DEBIT	CREDIT	
1							1
2							2
3							3
4							4
5							5
6							6
7							7
8							8
9							9

Supporting calculations for the bonus:

EXERCISE 12-13, Concluded

(2)

JOURNAL PAGE

	DATE		DESCRIPTION	POST. REF.	DEBIT	CREDIT	
1							1
2							2
3							3
4							4
5							5
6							6
7							7
8							8
9							9

Supporting calculations for the bonus:

EXERCISE 12-14

a.

JOURNAL PAGE

	DATE		DESCRIPTION	POST. REF.	DEBIT	CREDIT	
1							1
2							2
3							3
4							4
5							5

EXERCISE 12-14, Continued

b. (1)

JOURNAL PAGE

	DATE		DESCRIPTION	POST. REF.	DEBIT	CREDIT	
1							1
2							2
3							3
4							4
5							5
6							6
7							7
8							8

Supporting calculations for the bonus:

EXERCISE 12-14, Concluded

(2)

JOURNAL

PAGE

	DATE		DESCRIPTION	POST. REF.	DEBIT	CREDIT	
1							1
2							2
3							3
4							4
5							5
6							6
7							7
8							8

Supporting calculations for the bonus:

Name ______________________________

EXERCISE 12-15

Statement of Partnership Equity

	DENNIS OVERTON, CAPITAL	BEN TESTERMAN, CAPITAL	RANDY CAMPBELL, CAPITAL	TOTAL PARTNERSHIP CAPITAL

Calculations

Admission of Randy Campbell:

EXERCISE 12-15, Concluded

Net income distribution:

Withdrawals:

EXERCISE 12-16

a. and b.

JOURNAL

PAGE

	DATE		DESCRIPTION	POST. REF.	DEBIT	CREDIT	
1							1
2							2
3							3
4							4
5							5
6							6
7							7
8							8
9							9
10							10
11							11
12							12
13							13
14							14
15							15
16							16
17							17
18							18

EXERCISE 12-17

a. through f.

Name ______________________________

EXERCISE 12-17, Concluded

EXERCISE 12-18

a.

b. and c.

	HEWITT	PATEL

EXERCISE 12-19

	OLIVER	ANSARI	TOTAL

EXERCISE 12-20

a. ______________________

b. ______________________

____

c.

JOURNAL PAGE

	DATE		DESCRIPTION	POST. REF.	DEBIT	CREDIT	
1							1
2							2
3							3

Supporting calculations:

	LEWIS	ZAPATA	FOWLER

EXERCISE 12-21

a. ____

b.

	BRAY	LINCOLN	MAPES	TOTAL

c.

	BRAY	LINCOLN	MAPES	TOTAL

EXERCISE 12-22

	NETTLES	KING	TANAKA

Name ______________________

EXERCISE 12-23

Statement of Partnership Liquidation

						CAPITAL	
	CASH	+ NONCASH ASSETS	= LIABILITIES	+ GOLD	+ PORTER	+ SIMS	

EXERCISE 12-24

a.

Statement of LLC Liquidation

							MEMBER EQUITY				
	CASH	+	NONCASH ASSETS	=	LIABILITIES	+	LESTER	+	TORRES	+	HEARST

EXERCISE 12-24, Concluded

b.

JOURNAL

PAGE

	DATE		DESCRIPTION	POST. REF.	DEBIT	CREDIT	
1							1
2							2
3							3
4							4
5							5
6							6
7							7

c. ____

Name ______________________________

EXERCISE 12-25

a.

JOURNAL PAGE

	DATE		DESCRIPTION	POST. REF.	DEBIT	CREDIT	
1							1
2							2
3							3
4							4
5							5
6							6
7							7
8							8
9							9
10							10
11							11
12							12
13							13
14							14
15							15

b.

Statement of Partnership Equity

	ANGEL ALVAREZ	EMMA ALLISON	TOTAL

EXERCISE 12-26

a.

b.

EXERCISE 12-27

a. ______________________________

b. ______________________________

This Page Not Used.

Name ______________________________

PROBLEM 12-1 ___

1.

JOURNAL PAGE

	DATE		DESCRIPTION	POST. REF.	DEBIT	CREDIT	
1							1
2							2
3							3
4							4
5							5
6							6
7							7
8							8
9							9
10							10
11							11
12							12
13							13
14							14
15							15
16							16
17							17
18							18

PROBLEM 12-1 ___, Continued

2.

Balance Sheet

Name ____________________________________

PROBLEM 12-1 ___, Concluded

3.

JOURNAL

PAGE ______

	DATE		DESCRIPTION	POST. REF.	DEBIT	CREDIT	
1							1
2							2
3							3
4							4
5							5
6							6
7							7
8							8
9							9
10							10
11							11
12							12
13							13
14							14

Computations:

This Page Not Used.

PROBLEM 12-2 ___

Plan	(1) Net Income of ___________		(2) Net Income of ___________	
	Partner: ___________	Partner: ___________	Partner: ___________	Partner: ___________
a.				
b.				
c.				
d.				
e.				
f.				

PROBLEM 12-2 ___, Concluded

Supporting calculations:

	NET INCOME OF ____________		NET INCOME OF ____________	

PROBLEM 12-3 ___

1.

Income Statement

Division of net income:

PROBLEM 12-3 ___, Continued

2.

Statement of Partnership Equity

Name ________________________________

PROBLEM 12-3 ___, Concluded

3.

Balance Sheet

This Page Not Used.

Name ____________________

PROBLEM 12-4 ___

1. and 2.

JOURNAL

PAGE

DATE		DESCRIPTION	POST. REF.	DEBIT	CREDIT

PROBLEM 12-4 ___, Concluded

3.

Balance Sheet

PROBLEM 12-5 ___

1.

Statement of Partnership Liquidation

					CAPITAL	
	CASH +	NONCASH ASSETS =	LIABILITIES +	______ +	______ +	______

PROBLEM 12-5___, Concluded

2. a.

JOURNAL PAGE

	DATE		DESCRIPTION	POST. REF.	DEBIT	CREDIT	
1							1
2							2
3							3
4							4
5							5
6							6
7							7

b.

JOURNAL PAGE

	DATE		DESCRIPTION	POST. REF.	DEBIT	CREDIT	
1							1
2							2
3							3
4							4
5							5
6							6
7							7

PROBLEM 12-6 ___

1. a.

Statement of Partnership Liquidation

	CASH	+ NONCASH ASSETS	= LIABILITIES	+ CAPITAL ______	+ ______	+ ______

PROBLEM 12-6 ___, Continued

b.

Statement of Partnership Liquidation

	CASH	+ NONCASH ASSETS	= LIABILITIES	+ CAPITAL ______	+ CAPITAL ______	+ CAPITAL ______

PROBLEM 12-6 ___, Concluded

2. a.

JOURNAL

PAGE

	DATE		DESCRIPTION	POST. REF.	DEBIT	CREDIT	
1							1
2							2
3							3
4							4
5							5
6							6
7							7

b.

JOURNAL

PAGE

	DATE		DESCRIPTION	POST. REF.	DEBIT	CREDIT	
1							1
2							2
3							3
4							4
5							5
6							6
7							7

This Page Not Used.

Name ______________________________

EXERCISE 13-1

Description	1st Year	2nd Year	3rd Year	4th Year
Total dividend declared				
Preferred dividend (current)				
Preferred dividend in arrears				
Total preferred dividends				
Preferred shares outstanding				
Preferred dividend per share				
Dividend for common shares				
Common shares outstanding				
Common dividend per share				

EXERCISE 13-2

Description	1st Year	2nd Year	3rd Year	4th Year
Total dividend declared				
Preferred dividend (current)				
Preferred dividend in arrears				
Total preferred dividends				
Preferred shares outstanding				
Preferred dividend per share				
Dividend for common shares				
Common shares outstanding				
Common dividend per share				

EXERCISE 13-3

a.

JOURNAL

PAGE

	DATE		DESCRIPTION	POST. REF.	DEBIT	CREDIT	
1							1
2							2
3							3
4							4
5							5
6							6
7							7
8							8
9							9
10							10
11							11
12							12
13							13
14							14
15							15
16							16
17							17
18							18

b. ____

Name ______________________

EXERCISE 13-4

a.

JOURNAL

PAGE

	DATE		DESCRIPTION	POST. REF.	DEBIT	CREDIT	
1							1
2							2
3							3
4							4
5							5
6							6
7							7
8							8
9							9
10							10
11							11
12							12
13							13
14							14
15							15
16							16
17							17
18							18

b. ______________________

EXERCISE 13-5

JOURNAL PAGE

	DATE		DESCRIPTION	POST. REF.	DEBIT	CREDIT	
1							1
2							2
3							3
4							4
5							5
6							6
7							7
8							8

EXERCISE 13-6

a., b., and c.

JOURNAL PAGE

	DATE		DESCRIPTION	POST. REF.	DEBIT	CREDIT	
1							1
2							2
3							3
4							4
5							5
6							6
7							7
8							8
9							9
10							10
11							11
12							12
13							13
14							14
15							15
16							16
17							17
18							18
19							19
20							20

Name ______________________________

EXERCISE 13-7

JOURNAL

PAGE

	DATE		DESCRIPTION	POST. REF.	DEBIT	CREDIT	
1							1
2							2
3							3
4							4
5							5
6							6
7							7
8							8
9							9
10							10
11							11
12							12
13							13
14							14
15							15
16							16
17							17
18							18

EXERCISE 13-8

JOURNAL

PAGE

	DATE		DESCRIPTION	POST. REF.	DEBIT	CREDIT	
1							1
2							2
3							3
4							4
5							5
6							6
7							7
8							8
9							9
10							10
11							11
12							12
13							13
14							14
15							15
16							16
17							17
18							18
19							19
20							20
21							21
22							22
23							23
24							24
25							25
26							26
27							27
28							28

Name ______________________________

EXERCISE 13-9

JOURNAL PAGE

	DATE		DESCRIPTION	POST. REF.	DEBIT	CREDIT	
1							1
2							2
3							3
4							4
5							5
6							6
7							7
8							8
9							9

EXERCISE 13-10

a.

JOURNAL PAGE

	DATE		DESCRIPTION	POST. REF.	DEBIT	CREDIT	
1							1
2							2
3							3
4							4
5							5
6							6
7							7
8							8
9							9
10							10
11							11
12							12

b. (1) Total paid-in capital: ______________________________

(2) Total retained earnings: ______________________________

(3) Total stockholders' equity: ______________________________

c. (1) Total paid-in capital: ______________________________

(2) Total retained earnings: ______________________________

(3) Total stockholders' equity: ______________________________

EXERCISE 13-11

a. ______________________________

b. ______________________________

EXERCISE 13-12

	Assets	Liabilities	Stockholders' Equity
(1) Authorizing and issuing stock certificates in a stock split	______	______	______
(2) Declaring a stock dividend..............................	______	______	______
(3) Issuing stock certificates for the stock dividend declared in (2)	______	______	______
(4) Declaring a cash dividend	______	______	______
(5) Paying the cash dividend declared in (4)........	______	______	______

Name ______________________________

EXERCISE 13-13

JOURNAL

PAGE

	DATE		DESCRIPTION	POST. REF.	DEBIT	CREDIT	
1							1
2							2
3							3
4							4
5							5
6							6
7							7
8							8
9							9
10							10
11							11
12							12
13							13
14							14
15							15
16							16
17							17
18							18
19							19
20							20
21							21
22							22
23							23
24							24
25							25
26							26
27							27
28							28
29							29
30							30
31							31
32							32
33							33
34							34
35							35
36							36

EXERCISE 13-14

a.

JOURNAL PAGE

	DATE	DESCRIPTION	POST. REF.	DEBIT	CREDIT	
1						1
2						2
3						3
4						4
5						5
6						6
7						7
8						8
9						9
10						10
11						11
12						12
13						13
14						14
15						15
16						16
17						17
18						18
19						19
20						20
21						21
22						22

b. ____

c. ____

EXERCISE 13-15

a.

JOURNAL PAGE

DATE		DESCRIPTION	POST. REF.	DEBIT	CREDIT

b. ______________________

c. ______________________

d. ______________________

EXERCISE 13-16

a.

JOURNAL

PAGE

	DATE		DESCRIPTION	POST. REF.	DEBIT	CREDIT	
1							1
2							2
3							3
4							4
5							5
6							6
7							7
8							8
9							9
10							10
11							11
12							12
13							13
14							14
15							15
16							16
17							17
18							18
19							19
20							20
21							21
22							22

b. ______________________________

c. ______________________________

d. ______________________________

____

____

____

____

____

EXERCISE 13-17

EXERCISE 13-18

EXERCISE 13-19

EXERCISE 13-20

Retained Earnings Statement

EXERCISE 13-21

EXERCISE 13-21, Concluded

(Optional)

EXERCISE 13-22

Statement of Stockholders' Equity

EXERCISE 13-23

EXERCISE 13-24

a.

b.

	YEAR 3	YEAR 2	YEAR 1

EXERCISE 13-24, Concluded

EXERCISE 13-25

a. Caterpillar Inc.:

Deere & Company:

b.

Name ______________________________

PROBLEM 13-1 ___

1.

Year	Total Dividends	Preferred Dividends		Common Dividends	
		Total	Per Share	Total	Per Share
Year 1					
Year 2					
Year 3					
Year 4					
Year 5					
Year 6					

2. Average annual dividend for preferred: ______________________________

   Average annual dividend for common: ______________________________

3. a. ______________________________

   b. ______________________________

This Page Not Used.

PROBLEM 13-2 ___

JOURNAL

PAGE

	DATE		DESCRIPTION	POST. REF.	DEBIT	CREDIT	
1							1
2							2
3							3
4							4
5							5
6							6
7							7
8							8
9							9
10							10
11							11
12							12
13							13
14							14
15							15
16							16
17							17
18							18
19							19
20							20
21							21
22							22
23							23
24							24
25							25
26							26
27							27
28							28
29							29
30							30
31							31
32							32
33							33
34							34
35							35
36							36

This Page Not Used.

Name ______________________________

PROBLEM 13-3 ___

a. through g.

JOURNAL

PAGE

DATE		DESCRIPTION	POST. REF.	DEBIT	CREDIT

PROBLEM 13-3 ___, Concluded

JOURNAL

PAGE

DATE		DESCRIPTION	POST. REF.	DEBIT	CREDIT

Name ______________________________

PROBLEM 13-4 ___

1. and 2.

Common Stock

Paid-In Capital in Excess of Stated Value—Common Stock

Retained Earnings

Treasury Stock

PROBLEM 13-4 ___, Continued

Paid-In Capital from Sale of Treasury Stock

Stock Dividends Distributable

Stock Dividends

Cash Dividends

Name ______________________________

PROBLEM 13-4 ___, Continued

2.

JOURNAL PAGE ____

	DATE		DESCRIPTION	POST. REF.	DEBIT	CREDIT	
1							1
2							2
3							3
4							4
5							5
6							6
7							7
8							8
9							9
10							10
11							11
12							12
13							13
14							14
15							15
16							16
17							17
18							18
19							19
20							20
21							21
22							22
23							23
24							24
25							25
26							26
27							27
28							28
29							29
30							30
31							31
32							32
33							33
34							34
35							35

PROBLEM 13-4 ___, Continued

JOURNAL

PAGE

	DATE		DESCRIPTION	POST. REF.	DEBIT	CREDIT	
1							1
2							2
3							3
4							4
5							5
6							6
7							7
8							8
9							9
10							10
11							11
12							12
13							13
14							14
15							15
16							16
17							17
18							18
19							19
20							20
21							21
22							22
23							23
24							24
25							25
26							26
27							27
28							28
29							29
30							30
31							31
32							32
33							33
34							34
35							35
36							36

Name ______________________________

PROBLEM 13-4 ___, Concluded

3.

Retained Earnings Statement

4.

This Page Not Used.

Name ______________________________

PROBLEM 13-5 ___

JOURNAL

PAGE

	DATE		DESCRIPTION	POST. REF.	DEBIT	CREDIT	
1							1
2							2
3							3
4							4
5							5
6							6
7							7
8							8
9							9
10							10
11							11
12							12
13							13
14							14
15							15
16							16
17							17
18							18
19							19
20							20
21							21
22							22
23							23
24							24
25							25
26							26
27							27
28							28
29							29
30							30
31							31
32							32
33							33
34							34
35							35
36							36

PROBLEM 13-5 ___, Concluded

JOURNAL

PAGE

DATE		DESCRIPTION	POST. REF.	DEBIT	CREDIT

Name ________________________________

EXERCISE 14-1

	a.	b.	c.
Earnings before bond interest and income tax	$	$	$
Bond interest			
Balance	$	$	$
Income tax			
Net income	$	$	$
Dividends on preferred stock			
Earnings available for common stock	$	$	$
Shares of common stock outstanding			
Earnings per share on common stock	$	$	$

EXERCISE 14-2

EXERCISE 14-3

EXERCISE 14-4

EXERCISE 14-5

JOURNAL PAGE

	DATE		DESCRIPTION	POST. REF.	DEBIT	CREDIT	
1							1
2							2
3							3
4							4
5							5
6							6
7							7
8							8
9							9
10							10

EXERCISE 14-6

a. 1. through 3.

JOURNAL PAGE

	DATE		DESCRIPTION	POST. REF.	DEBIT	CREDIT	
1							1
2							2
3							3
4							4
5							5
6							6
7							7
8							8
9							9
10							10
11							11
12							12
13							13
14							14

b.

Name ______________________________

EXERCISE 14-6, Concluded

c. ______________________________

EXERCISE 14-7

a. and b.

JOURNAL PAGE

	DATE		DESCRIPTION	POST. REF.	DEBIT	CREDIT	
1							1
2							2
3							3
4							4
5							5
6							6
7							7
8							8
9							9
10							10
11							11
12							12

c. ______________________________

EXERCISE 14-8

JOURNAL

PAGE

	DATE		DESCRIPTION	POST. REF.	DEBIT	CREDIT	
1							1
2							2
3							3
4							4
5							5
6							6
7							7
8							8
9							9
10							10
11							11
12							12
13							13
14							14

EXERCISE 14-9

JOURNAL

PAGE

	DATE		DESCRIPTION	POST. REF.	DEBIT	CREDIT	
1							1
2							2
3							3
4							4
5							5
6							6
7							7
8							8
9							9
10							10
11							11
12							12
13							13
14							14

EXERCISE 14-10

a. 1. and 2.

JOURNAL

PAGE

	DATE		DESCRIPTION	POST. REF.	DEBIT	CREDIT	
1							1
2							2
3							3
4							4
5							5
6							6
7							7
8							8

EXERCISE 14-10, Concluded

b.

Supporting Calculations:

Name ______________________________

EXERCISE 14-11

JOURNAL

PAGE

	DATE		DESCRIPTION	POST. REF.	DEBIT	CREDIT	
1							1
2							2
3							3
4							4
5							5
6							6
7							7
8							8
9							9
10							10
11							11
12							12
13							13
14							14

EXERCISE 14-12

a.

Amortization of Installment Notes					
	A	B	C	D	E
For the Year Ending December 31	January 1 Carrying Amount	Note Payment (Cash Paid)	Interest Expense (7% of January 1 Note Carrying Amount)	Decrease in Notes Payable (B – C)	December 31 Carrying Amount (A – D)

EXERCISE 14-12, Concluded

b.

JOURNAL

PAGE

DATE		DESCRIPTION	POST. REF.	DEBIT	CREDIT

c. ____

____

Name ______________________________

EXERCISE 14-13

1. ______________________________

2. ______________________________

EXERCISE 14-14

a. Current year: ______________________________

Prior year: ______________________________

b. ______________________________

EXERCISE 14-15

a. Current year:

Prior year:

b.

EXERCISE 14-16

a. Current year:

Prior year:

b.

Name ____________________

APPENDIX 1 EXERCISE 14-17

a. ____________________

b. ____________________

APPENDIX 1 EXERCISE 14-18

a.

b. ____________________

c. ____________________

APPENDIX 1 EXERCISE 14-19

____

APPENDIX 1 EXERCISE 14-20

____

APPENDIX 1 EXERCISE 14-21

APPENDIX 1 EXERCISE 14-22

APPENDIX 2 EXERCISE 14-23

a. 1. through 3.

JOURNAL PAGE

	DATE		DESCRIPTION	POST. REF.	DEBIT	CREDIT	
1							1
2							2
3							3
4							4
5							5
6							6
7							7
8							8
9							9
10							10
11							11
12							12
13							13
14							14
15							15
16							16
17							17
18							18

b.

c. ______________________________

APPENDIX 2 EXERCISE 14-24

a. 1. through 3.

JOURNAL

PAGE

	DATE		DESCRIPTION	POST. REF.	DEBIT	CREDIT	
1							1
2							2
3							3
4							4
5							5
6							6
7							7
8							8
9							9
10							10
11							11
12							12
13							13
14							14
15							15
16							16
17							17
18							18

b.

c.

Name ______________________________

APPENDIX 1 AND APPENDIX 2 EXERCISE 14-25

a. through d.

APPENDIX 1 AND APPENDIX 2 EXERCISE 14-26

a. through d.

Name ______________________________

PROBLEM 14-1 ___

1.

	Plan 1	Plan 2	Plan 3
Earnings before interest and income tax	$	$	$
Interest on bonds			
Income before income tax	$	$	$
Income tax			
Net income	$	$	$
Dividends on preferred stock			
Available for dividends on common stock	$	$	$
Shares of common stock outstanding			
Earnings per share on common stock	$	$	$

2.

	Plan 1	Plan 2	Plan 3
Earnings before interest and income tax	$	$	$
Interest on bonds			
Income before income tax	$	$	$
Income tax			
Net income	$	$	$
Dividends on preferred stock			
Available for dividends on common stock	$	$	$
Shares of common stock outstanding			
Earnings per share on common stock	$	$	$

PROBLEM 14-1 ___, Concluded

3. ______________________________

PROBLEM 14-2 ___

1. and 2.

JOURNAL

PAGE ____

DATE		DESCRIPTION	POST. REF.	DEBIT	CREDIT

PROBLEM 14-2 ___, Concluded

3. ______________________

4. ______________________

5.

Name ______________________

PROBLEM 14-3 ___

1. and 2.

JOURNAL

PAGE

	DATE		DESCRIPTION	POST. REF.	DEBIT	CREDIT	
1							1
2							2
3							3
4							4
5							5
6							6
7							7
8							8
9							9
10							10
11							11
12							12
13							13
14							14
15							15
16							16
17							17
18							18
19							19
20							20
21							21
22							22

PROBLEM 14-3 ___, Concluded

3. ____________________

4. ____________________

5.

Name ______________________________

PROBLEM 14-4 ___

1.

JOURNAL PAGE

	DATE		DESCRIPTION	POST. REF.	DEBIT	CREDIT	
1							1
2							2
3							3
4							4
5							5
6							6
7							7
8							8
9							9
10							10
11							11
12							12
13							13
14							14
15							15
16							16
17							17
18							18
19							19
20							20
21							21
22							22
23							23
24							24
25							25
26							26
27							27
28							28
29							29
30							30
31							31
32							32
33							33
34							34
35							35

PROBLEM 14-4 ___, Concluded

JOURNAL

PAGE

	DATE		DESCRIPTION	POST. REF.	DEBIT	CREDIT	
1							1
2							2
3							3
4							4
5							5
6							6
7							7
8							8
9							9
10							10
11							11
12							12
13							13
14							14
15							15
16							16
17							17
18							18
19							19
20							20
21							21
22							22
23							23
24							24

2. (a) Year 1: ______________________

(b) Year 2: ______________________

3.

Name ______________________________

APPENDIX 1 AND APPENDIX 2 PROBLEM 14-5 ___

1. and 2.

JOURNAL

PAGE

	DATE		DESCRIPTION	POST. REF.	DEBIT	CREDIT	
1							1
2							2
3							3
4							4
5							5
6							6
7							7
8							8
9							9
10							10
11							11
12							12
13							13
14							14
15							15
16							16
17							17
18							18
19							19
20							20
21							21
22							22

3. ______________________________

This Page Not Used.

Name ______________________

APPENDIX 1 AND APPENDIX 2 PROBLEM 14-6 ___

1. and 2.

JOURNAL

PAGE

	DATE		DESCRIPTION	POST. REF.	DEBIT	CREDIT	
1							1
2							2
3							3
4							4
5							5
6							6
7							7
8							8
9							9
10							10
11							11
12							12
13							13
14							14
15							15
16							16
17							17
18							18
19							19
20							20
21							21
22							22

3. ____

This Page Not Used.

EXERCISE 15-1

a. through d.

JOURNAL

PAGE

	DATE		DESCRIPTION	POST. REF.	DEBIT	CREDIT	
1							1
2							2
3							3
4							4
5							5
6							6
7							7
8							8
9							9
10							10
11							11
12							12
13							13
14							14
15							15
16							16
17							17
18							18
19							19
20							20
21							21
22							22
23							23
24							24

EXERCISE 15-2

a. through d.

JOURNAL

PAGE

	DATE		DESCRIPTION	POST. REF.	DEBIT	CREDIT	
1							1
2							2
3							3
4							4
5							5
6							6
7							7
8							8
9							9
10							10
11							11
12							12
13							13
14							14
15							15
16							16
17							17
18							18
19							19
20							20
21							21
22							22
23							23
24							24
25							25
26							26
27							27
28							28

Name ______________________________

EXERCISE 15-3

a. through d.

JOURNAL

PAGE ______

	DATE		DESCRIPTION	POST. REF.	DEBIT	CREDIT	
1							1
2							2
3							3
4							4
5							5
6							6
7							7
8							8
9							9
10							10
11							11
12							12
13							13
14							14
15							15
16							16
17							17
18							18
19							19
20							20
21							21
22							22
23							23
24							24
25							25
26							26
27							27
28							28
29							29
30							30
31							31
32							32
33							33
34							34
35							35

EXERCISE 15-4

a. and b.

JOURNAL

PAGE

DATE		DESCRIPTION	POST. REF.	DEBIT	CREDIT

Name ______________________________

EXERCISE 15-5

EXERCISE 15-6

a., b., and c.

JOURNAL

PAGE

	DATE		DESCRIPTION	POST. REF.	DEBIT	CREDIT	
1							1
2							2
3							3
4							4
5							5
6							6
7							7
8							8
9							9
10							10
11							11
12							12
13							13
14							14
15							15
16							16
17							17
18							18
19							19
20							20

EXERCISE 15-7

JOURNAL

PAGE

DATE		DESCRIPTION	POST. REF.	DEBIT	CREDIT

Name ______________________________

EXERCISE 15-8

JOURNAL

PAGE ____

	DATE		DESCRIPTION	POST. REF.	DEBIT	CREDIT	
1							1
2							2
3							3
4							4
5							5
6							6
7							7
8							8
9							9
10							10
11							11
12							12
13							13
14							14
15							15
16							16
17							17
18							18
19							19
20							20
21							21
22							22
23							23
24							24
25							25
26							26
27							27
28							28
29							29
30							30
31							31
32							32
33							33
34							34
35							35
36							36

EXERCISE 15-9

JOURNAL

PAGE

DATE		DESCRIPTION	POST. REF.	DEBIT	CREDIT

EXERCISE 15-10

a. (1) and (2)

JOURNAL PAGE

	DATE		DESCRIPTION	POST. REF.	DEBIT	CREDIT	
1							1
2							2
3							3
4							4
5							5
6							6
7							7
8							8
9							9
10							10
11							11
12							12
13							13
14							14

b. ______________________________

EXERCISE 15-11

a.

JOURNAL

PAGE

	DATE		DESCRIPTION	POST. REF.	DEBIT	CREDIT	
1							1
2							2
3							3
4							4
5							5
6							6
7							7
8							8
9							9
10							10
11							11
12							12
13							13
14							14
15							15
16							16
17							17
18							18
19							19
20							20
21							21
22							22

b.

Name ______________________________

EXERCISE 15-12

a.

JOURNAL PAGE

	DATE		DESCRIPTION	POST. REF.	DEBIT	CREDIT	
1							1
2							2
3							3
4							4
5							5
6							6
7							7
8							8
9							9
10							10
11							11
12							12
13							13
14							14
15							15
16							16
17							17
18							18

b.

EXERCISE 15-12, Concluded

c.

EXERCISE 15-13

Name ______________________________

EXERCISE 15-14

JED Capital Inc.

Selected Income Statement Items

For the Years Ended December 31, Year 2 and Year 3

	Year 2	Year 3
Operating income	a. __________	e. __________
Unrealized gain (loss)	b. __________	$(11,000)
Net income	c. __________	28,000

JED Capital Inc.

Selected Balance Sheet Items

December 31, Year 1, Year 2, and Year 3

	Dec. 31, Year 1	Dec. 31, Year 2	Dec. 31, Year 3
Trading investments, at cost	$144,000	$168,000	$205,000
Valuation allowance for trading investments	(12,000)	17,000	g. __________
Trading investments, at fair value	d. __________	f. __________	h. __________
Retained earnings	$210,000	$245,000	i. __________

EXERCISE 15-15

a.

JOURNAL

PAGE

	DATE		DESCRIPTION	POST. REF.	DEBIT	CREDIT	
1							1
2							2
3							3
4							4
5							5
6							6
7							7
8							8
9							9
10							10
11							11
12							12
13							13
14							14
15							15
16							16
17							17
18							18

b.

Name ____________________

EXERCISE 15-16

a. and b.

JOURNAL PAGE

	DATE		DESCRIPTION	POST. REF.	DEBIT	CREDIT	
1							1
2							2
3							3
4							4
5							5
6							6
7							7
8							8
9							9
10							10
11							11
12							12
13							13
14							14
15							15
16							16
17							17
18							18

EXERCISE 15-17

a.

JOURNAL

PAGE

	DATE		DESCRIPTION	POST. REF.	DEBIT	CREDIT	
1							1
2							2
3							3
4							4
5							5

Computations:

b.

EXERCISE 15-18

a. and b.

EXERCISE 15-19

Highland Industries Inc.
Selected Income Statement Items
For the Years Ended December 31, Year 2 and Year 3

	Year 2	Year 3
Operating income	a. ________	g. ________
Gain (loss) from sale of investments	$7,500	$(12,000)
Net income (loss)	b. ________	(21,000)

Highland Industries Inc.
Selected Balance Sheet Items
December 31, Year 1, Year 2, and Year 3

	Dec. 31, Year 1	Dec. 31, Year 2	Dec. 31, Year 3
Assets			
Available-for-sale investments, at cost	$ 90,000	$ 86,000	$102,000
Valuation allowance for available-for-sale investments	12,000	(11,000)	h. ________
Available-for-sale investments, at fair value	c. ________	e. ________	i. ________
Stockholders' Equity			
Unrealized gain (loss) on available-for-sale investments	d. ________	f. ________	(16,400)
Retained earnings	$175,400	$220,000	j. ________

Name ______________________________

EXERCISE 15-20

a.

JOURNAL PAGE

	DATE		DESCRIPTION	POST. REF.	DEBIT	CREDIT	
1							1
2							2
3							3
4							4
5							5
6							6
7							7
8							8
9							9
10							10
11							11
12							12
13							13
14							14
15							15

b. ______________________________

EXERCISE 15-21

a. (1) and (2)

JOURNAL

PAGE

	DATE		DESCRIPTION	POST. REF.	DEBIT	CREDIT	
1							1
2							2
3							3
4							4
5							5
6							6
7							7
8							8
9							9
10							10
11							11
12							12
13							13
14							14
15							15

b. ____

Name ______________________

EXERCISE 15-22

a.

JOURNAL PAGE

	DATE		DESCRIPTION	POST. REF.	DEBIT	CREDIT	
1							1
2							2
3							3
4							4
5							5
6							6
7							7

Computations:

b. ______________________

EXERCISE 15-23

a.

Balance Sheet (selected items)

b.

Balance Sheet (selected items)

Name ________________________________

EXERCISE 15-24

Balance Sheet (selected Stockholders' Equity items)

EXERCISE 15-25

____

____

____

____

____

EXERCISE 15-26

a. Current year: ______________________________

Previous year: ______________________________

b. ____

EXERCISE 15-27

APPENDIX EXERCISE 15-28

APPENDIX EXERCISE 15-29

PROBLEM 15-1 ___

1.

JOURNAL

PAGE

	DATE		DESCRIPTION	POST. REF.	DEBIT	CREDIT	
1							1
2							2
3							3
4							4
5							5
6							6
7							7
8							8
9							9
10							10
11							11
12							12
13							13
14							14
15							15
16							16
17							17
18							18
19							19
20							20
21							21
22							22
23							23
24							24
25							25
26							26
27							27
28							28
29							29
30							30
31							31
32							32
33							33
34							34
35							35

PROBLEM 15-1 ___, Concluded

JOURNAL

PAGE

	DATE		DESCRIPTION	POST. REF.	DEBIT	CREDIT	
1							1
2							2
3							3
4							4
5							5
6							6
7							7
8							8
9							9
10							10
11							11
12							12
13							13
14							14
15							15
16							16
17							17
18							18

2. ____

Name ______________________________

PROBLEM 15-2 ___

1.

JOURNAL PAGE

	DATE		DESCRIPTION	POST. REF.	DEBIT	CREDIT	
1							1
2							2
3							3
4							4
5							5
6							6
7							7
8							8
9							9
10							10
11							11
12							12
13							13
14							14
15							15
16							16
17							17
18							18
19							19
20							20
21							21
22							22
23							23
24							24
25							25

Calculations:

PROBLEM 15-2 ___, Continued

JOURNAL

PAGE

DATE		DESCRIPTION	POST. REF.	DEBIT	CREDIT

PROBLEM 15-2 ___, Concluded

2.

Balance Sheet (selected items)

3. ______________________________

This Page Not Used.

Name ______________________________

PROBLEM 15-3 ___

1.

JOURNAL

PAGE

DATE		DESCRIPTION	POST. REF.	DEBIT	CREDIT

PROBLEM 15-3 ___, Continued

JOURNAL

PAGE

DATE		DESCRIPTION	POST. REF.	DEBIT	CREDIT

PROBLEM 15-3 ___, Concluded

2.

Balance Sheet (selected items)

This Page Not Used.

Name ______________________________

PROBLEM 15-4 ___

a. ______________________________

b. ______________________________

c. ______________________________

d. ______________________________

e. ______________________________

f. ______________________________

g. ______________________________

h. ______________________________

i. ______________________________

Calculations:

PROBLEM 15-4 ___, Continued

Completed comparative unclassified balance sheet (optional):

Balance Sheet

	DEC. 31, YEAR 2	DEC. 31, YEAR 1

Name ______________________________

PROBLEM 15-4 ___, Concluded

Calculations:

This Page Not Used.

COMPREHENSIVE PROBLEM 4, Continued

JOURNAL

PAGE

DATE		DESCRIPTION	POST. REF.	DEBIT	CREDIT

COMPREHENSIVE PROBLEM 4, Continued

JOURNAL

PAGE

	DATE		DESCRIPTION	POST. REF.	DEBIT	CREDIT	
1							1
2							2
3							3
4							4
5							5
6							6
7							7
8							8
9							9
10							10
11							11
12							12
13							13
14							14
15							15
16							16
17							17
18							18
19							19
20							20
21							21
22							22
23							23
24							24
25							25
26							26
27							27
28							28
29							29
30							30
31							31
32							32
33							33
34							34
35							35
36							36

Name ______________________________

COMPREHENSIVE PROBLEM 4, Continued

2. a.

Income Statement

COMPREHENSIVE PROBLEM 4, Continued

Income Statement (continued)

COMPREHENSIVE PROBLEM 4, Continued

b.

Retained Earnings Statement

COMPREHENSIVE PROBLEM 4, Continued

c.

Balance Sheet

Name ____________________

COMPREHENSIVE PROBLEM 4, Continued

Balance Sheet (continued)

COMPREHENSIVE PROBLEM 4, Concluded

Balance Sheet (continued)

Name ______________________________

EXERCISE 16-1

____

EXERCISE 16-2

a. ______________________________
b. ______________________________
c. ______________________________
d. ______________________________
e. ______________________________
f. ______________________________
g. ______________________________
h. ______________________________

EXERCISE 16-3

a. Redeemed bonds: ______________________

b. Issued preferred stock: ______________________

c. Paid cash dividends: ______________________

d. Net income: ______________________

e. Sold equipment: ______________________

f. Purchased treasury stock: ______________________

g. Purchased patents: ______________________

h. Purchased buildings: ______________________

i. Sold long-term investments: ______________________

j. Issued bonds: ______________________

k. Issued common stock: ______________________

EXERCISE 16-4

a. Increase in merchandise inventory: ______________________

b. Increase in prepaid expenses: ______________________

c. Depreciation of fixed assets: ______________________

d. Gain on disposal of fixed assets: ______________________

e. Amortization of patent: ______________________

f. Increase in notes payable due in 120 days to vendors: ______________________

g. Increase in accounts payable: ______________________

h. Decrease in wages payable: ______________________

i. Decrease in notes receivable due in 60 days from customers: ______________________

j. Decrease in accounts receivable: ______________________

k. Loss on retirement of long-term debt: ______________________

Name ______________________________

EXERCISE 16-5

a.

b.

EXERCISE 16-6

a.

b.

Name ________________________________

EXERCISE 16-7

a.

b. ____

EXERCISE 16-8

EXERCISE 16-9

EXERCISE 16-10

EXERCISE 16-11

EXERCISE 16-12

EXERCISE 16-13

EXERCISE 16-14

Name ______________________________

EXERCISE 16-15

a.

b. ______________________________

EXERCISE 16-16

a.

b.

Name ______________________________

EXERCISE 16-17

a.

Statement of Cash Flows

EXERCISE 16-17, Concluded

b. ____

Name ______________________________

EXERCISE 16-18

a. ______________________________

EXERCISE 16-18, Continued

b.

Statement of Cash Flows

Name ____________________

EXERCISE 16-18, Concluded

Statement of Cash Flows (continued)

EXERCISE 16-19

a.

b.

EXERCISE 16-19, Concluded

c. ______________________________

EXERCISE 16-20

EXERCISE 16-21

a.

b.

Name ______________________________

EXERCISE 16-22

a.

Computations:

EXERCISE 16-22, Concluded

b.

Name ______________________________

EXERCISE 16-23

Computations:

EXERCISE 16-24

a.

b. ______________________

EXERCISE 16-25

a.

	RECENT FISCAL YEAR END (all numbers in thousands)

EXERCISE 16-25, Concluded

b. ____

____

____

____

____

____

____

c. ____

____

____

____

EXERCISE 16-26

This Page Not Used.

Name ______________________________

PROBLEM 16-1 ___

Statement of Cash Flows

PROBLEM 16-1 ___, Continued

Statement of Cash Flows (continued)

PROBLEM 16-1 ___, Continued

The use of this form is not required unless so indicated by the instructor.

	A	B	C	D	E
1					
2	**Spreadsheet (Work Sheet) for Statement of Cash Flows**				
3					
4		**Balance,**	**Transactions**		**Balance,**
5	**Account Title**	______	**Debit**	**Credit**	______
6					
7					
8					
9					
10					
11					
12					
13					
14					
15					
16					
17					
18					
19					
20					
21					
22					
23					
24					
25					
26					
27					
28					
29					
30					
31					
32					
33					
34					
35					
36					
37					
38					
39					
40					
41					
42					
43					
44					
45					

PROBLEM 16-1 ___, Concluded

	A	B	C	D	E
1					
2	Spreadsheet (Work Sheet) for Statement of Cash Flows (continued)				
3					
4		Balance,	Transactions		Balance,
5	Account Title	________	Debit	Credit	________
6					
7					
8					
9					
10					
11					
12					
13					
14					
15					
16					
17					
18					
19					
20					
21					
22					
23					
24					
25					
26					
27					
28					
29					
30					
31					
32					
33					
34					
35					
36					
37					
38					
39					
40					
41					
42					
43					
44					
45					

Name ______________________

PROBLEM 16-2 ___

Statement of Cash Flows

PROBLEM 16-2 ___, Continued

Statement of Cash Flows (continued)

Name ______________________________

PROBLEM 16-2 ___, Continued

The use of this form is not required unless so indicated by the instructor.

	A	B	C	D	E
1					
2	**Spreadsheet (Work Sheet) for Statement of Cash Flows**				
3					
4		**Balance,**	**Transactions**		**Balance,**
5	**Account Title**		**Debit**	**Credit**	
6					
7					
8					
9					
10					
11					
12					
13					
14					
15					
16					
17					
18					
19					
20					
21					
22					
23					
24					
25					
26					
27					
28					
29					
30					
31					
32					
33					
34					
35					
36					
37					
38					
39					
40					
41					
42					
43					
44					
45					

PROBLEM 16-2 ___, Concluded

	A	B	C	D	E
1					
2	Spreadsheet (Work Sheet) for Statement of Cash Flows (continued)				
3					
4		Balance,	Transactions		Balance,
5	Account Title	______	Debit	Credit	______
6					
7					
8					
9					
10					
11					
12					
13					
14					
15					
16					
17					
18					
19					
20					
21					
22					
23					
24					
25					
26					
27					
28					
29					
30					
31					
32					
33					
34					
35					
36					
37					
38					
39					
40					
41					
42					
43					
44					
45					

Name ______________________________

PROBLEM 16-3 ___

Statement of Cash Flows

PROBLEM 16-3 ___, Continued

Statement of Cash Flows (continued)

Name ______________________________

PROBLEM 16-3 ___, Continued

The use of this form is not required unless so indicated by the instructor.

	A	B	C	D	E
1					
2	**Spreadsheet (Work Sheet) for Statement of Cash Flows**				
3					
4		Balance,	Transactions		Balance,
5	Account Title	______	Debit	Credit	______
6					
7					
8					
9					
10					
11					
12					
13					
14					
15					
16					
17					
18					
19					
20					
21					
22					
23					
24					
25					
26					
27					
28					
29					
30					
31					
32					
33					
34					
35					
36					
37					
38					
39					
40					
41					
42					
43					
44					
45					

PROBLEM 16-3 ___, Concluded

	A	B	C	D	E
1					
2	Spreadsheet (Work Sheet) for Statement of Cash Flows (continued)				
3					
4		Balance,	Transactions		Balance,
5	Account Title		Debit	Credit	
6					
7					
8					
9					
10					
11					
12					
13					
14					
15					
16					
17					
18					
19					
20					
21					
22					
23					
24					
25					
26					
27					
28					
29					
30					
31					
32					
33					
34					
35					
36					
37					
38					
39					
40					
41					
42					
43					
44					
45					

Name ____________________

PROBLEM 16-4 ___

Statement of Cash Flows

PROBLEM 16-4 ___, Concluded

Computations:

Name ______________________________

PROBLEM 16-5 ___

Statement of Cash Flows

PROBLEM 16-5 ___, Concluded

Computations:

Name ______________________________

EXERCISE 17-1

a.

Comparative Income Statement

	CURRENT YEAR		PREVIOUS YEAR	
	AMOUNT	PERCENT	AMOUNT	PERCENT

b. ______________________________

EXERCISE 17-2

a.

Comparative Income Statement (in thousands of dollars)

	CURRENT YEAR		PRIOR YEAR	
	AMOUNT	PERCENT	AMOUNT	PERCENT

Name ______________________________

EXERCISE 17-2, Concluded

b. ______________________________

EXERCISE 17-3

a.

Common-Sized Income Statement

	TANNENHILL COMPANY		ELECTRONICS INDUSTRY AVERAGE
	AMOUNT	PERCENT	

b.

Name ______________________________

EXERCISE 17-4

Comparative Balance Sheet

	CURRENT YEAR		PREVIOUS YEAR	
	AMOUNT	PERCENT	AMOUNT	PERCENT

EXERCISE 17-5

a.

Comparative Income Statement

	CURRENT YEAR AMOUNT	PREVIOUS YEAR AMOUNT	INCREASE (DECREASE)	
			AMOUNT	PERCENT

EXERCISE 17-5, Concluded

b. ______________________________

EXERCISE 17-6

a. (1) Working Capital = ______________________________

Current Year: ______________________________

Previous Year: ______________________________

(2) Current Ratio = ______________________________

Current Year: ______________________________

Previous Year: ______________________________

(3) Quick Ratio = ______________________________

Current Year: ______________________________

Previous Year: ______________________________

b. ______________________________

EXERCISE 17-7

a. (1) Current Ratio = ______________________

____

Current Year: ______________________

____

Previous Year: ______________________

____

(2) Quick Ratio = ______________________

____

Current Year: ______________________

____

Previous Year: ______________________

____

b. ______________________

____

____

____

____

____

____

____

EXERCISE 17-8

a.

b.

Name ______________________________

EXERCISE 17-9

a. (1) Accounts Receivable Turnover = ______________________________

20Y3: ______________________________

20Y2: ______________________________

(2) Number of Days' Sales in Receivables = ______________________________

20Y3: ______________________________

20Y2: ______________________________

b. ______________________________

EXERCISE 17-10

a. (1) Accounts Receivable Turnover = ______________________________

Xavier: ______________________________

Lestrade: ______________________________

(2) Number of Days' Sales in Receivables = ______________________________

Xavier: ______________________________

Lestrade: ______________________________

EXERCISE 17-10, Concluded

b. ______________________

EXERCISE 17-11

a. (1) Inventory Turnover = ______________________

Current Year: ______________________

Previous Year: ______________________

(2) Number of Days' Sales in Inventory = ______________________

Current Year: ______________________

Previous Year: ______________________

b. ______________________

Name ______________________________

EXERCISE 17-12

a. (1) Inventory Turnover = ______________________________

QT: ______________________________

Elppa: ______________________________

(2) Number of Days' Sales in Inventory = ______________________________

QT: ______________________________

Elppa: ______________________________

b. ______________________________

EXERCISE 17-13

a. Ratio of Liabilities to Stockholders' Equity = ____________________

____

Current Year: ____________________

____

Previous Year: ____________________

____

b. Times Interest Earned = ____________________

____

Current Year: ____________________

____

Previous Year: ____________________

____

c. ____________________

____

____

____

____

____

____

____

EXERCISE 17-14

a. Ratio of Liabilities to Stockholders' Equity = ____________________

____

Hasbro: ____________________

____

Mattel, Inc.: ____________________

____

b. Times Interest Earned = ____________________

____

Hasbro: ____________________

____

Mattel, Inc.: ____________________

____

Name ______________________________

EXERCISE 17-14, Concluded

c. ______________________________

EXERCISE 17-15

a. Ratio of Liabilities to Stockholders' Equity = ______________________________

Mondelez: ______________________________

Hershey: ______________________________

b. Ratio of Fixed Assets to Long-Term Liabilities = ______________________________

Mondelez: ______________________________

Hershey: ______________________________

EXERCISE 17-15, Concluded

c. ______________________

EXERCISE 17-16

a. Asset Turnover = ______________________

YRC: ______________________

Union Pacific: ______________________

C.H. Robinson: ______________________

Name ______________________________

EXERCISE 17-16, Concluded

b. ____

EXERCISE 17-17

a. Return on Total Assets = ____________________

____

20Y7: ____________________

____

20Y6: ____________________

____

Return on Stockholders' Equity = ____________________

____

20Y7: ____________________

____

20Y6: ____________________

____

Return on Common Stockholders' Equity = ____________________

____

20Y7: ____________________

____

20Y6: ____________________

____

b. ____________________

Name ______________________________

EXERCISE 17-18

a. Return on Total Assets = ______________________________

____

Fiscal Year 3: ______________________________

____

Fiscal Year 2: ______________________________

____

b. Return on Stockholders' Equity = ______________________________

____

Fiscal Year 3: ______________________________

____

Fiscal Year 2: ______________________________

____

c. ______________________________

d. ______________________________

EXERCISE 17-19

a. Ratio of Fixed Assets to Long-Term Liabilities = ______________________

b. Ratio of Liabilities to Stockholders' Equity = ______________________

c. Asset Turnover = ______________________

d. Return on Total Assets = ______________________

e. Return on Stockholders' Equity = ______________________

f. Return on Common Stockholders' Equity = ______________________

Name ______________________________

EXERCISE 17-20

a. Times Interest Earned = ______________________________

b. Earnings per Share on Common Stock = ______________________________

c. Price-Earnings Ratio = ______________________________

d. Dividends per Share of Common Stock = ______________________________

e. Dividend Yield = ______________________________

EXERCISE 17-21

a. Earnings per Share = ____________________

b. Price-Earnings Ratio = ____________________

c. Dividends per Share = ____________________

d. Dividend Yield = ____________________

Name ______________________________

EXERCISE 17-22

a. Price-Earnings Ratio = ______________________________

Deere & Company: ______________________________

Alphabet (Google): ______________________________

The Coca-Cola Company: ______________________________

Dividend Yield = ______________________________

Deere & Company: ______________________________

Alphabet (Google): ______________________________

The Coca-Cola Company: ______________________________

b. ______________________________

APPENDIX EXERCISE 17-23

a. Earnings per share on income before discontinued operations:

Earnings Before Discontinued Operations per Share on Common Stock = ______________

b. Earnings per Share on Common Stock = ______________

Name ______________________________

APPENDIX EXERCISE 17-24

a.

Partial Income Statement

b.

Partial Income Statement

APPENDIX EXERCISE 17-25

a. ______________________

b. ______________________

Name ______________________________

PROBLEM 17-1 ___

1.

____

Comparative Income Statement

____

	20Y2	20Y1	INCREASE (DECREASE)	
			AMOUNT	PERCENT

2. ____

This Page Not Used.

Name ______________________________

PROBLEM 17-2 ___

1.

Comparative Income Statement

	20Y2		20Y1	
	AMOUNT	PERCENT	AMOUNT	PERCENT

2.

This Page Not Used.

Name ______________________________

PROBLEM 17-3 ___

1. a. Working Capital = ______________________________

b. Current Ratio = ______________________________

c. Quick Ratio = ______________________________

PROBLEM 17-3 ___, Concluded

2.

Transaction	Working Capital	Current Ratio	Quick Ratio
a.			
b.			
c.			
d.			
e.			
f.			
g.			
h.			
i.			
j.			

Supporting data:

Transaction	Current Assets	Quick Assets	Current Liabilities
a.			
b.			
c.			
d.			
e.			
f.			
g.			
h.			
i.			
j.			

Name ________________________________

PROBLEM 17-4 ___

1. through 18.

1. Working Capital: ____

Ratio	Numerator	Denominator	Calculated Value
2. Current ratio			
3. Quick ratio			
4. Accounts receivable turnover			
5. Number of days' sales in receivables			
6. Inventory turnover			
7. Number of days' sales in inventory			
8. Ratio of fixed assets to long-term liabilities			
9. Ratio of liabilities to stockholders' equity			
10. Times interest earned			
11. Asset turnover			
12. Return on total assets			
13. Return on stockholders' equity			
14. Return on common stockholders' equity			
15. Earnings per share on common stock			
16. Price-earnings ratio			
17. Dividends per share of common stock			
18. Dividend yield			

This Page Not Used.

PROBLEM 17-5 ___

1. a.

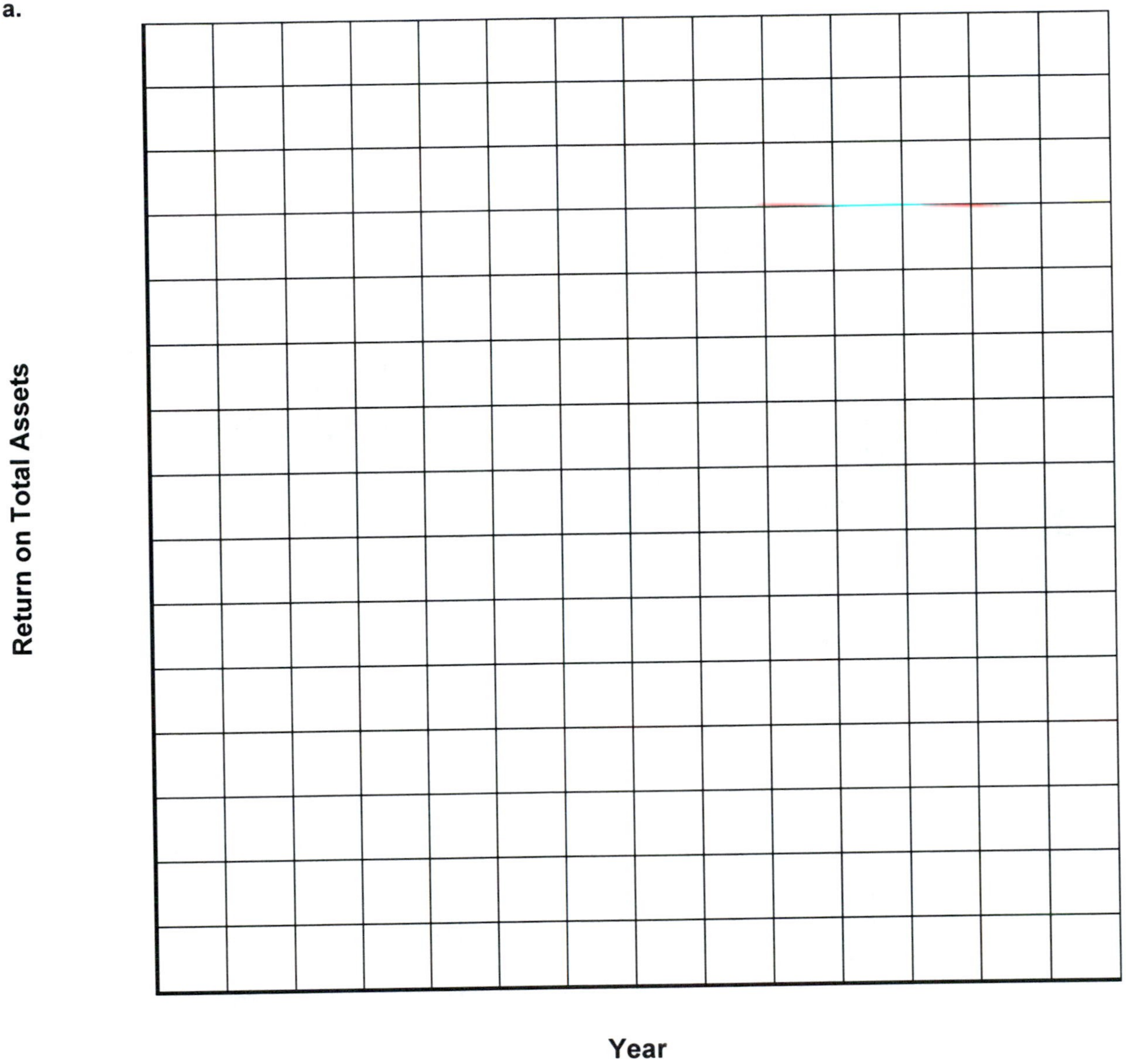

Return on Total Assets = ____________________

____

20Y8: ____________________

____

20Y7: ____________________

____

20Y6: ____________________

____

20Y5: ____________________

____

20Y4: ____________________

____

PROBLEM 17-5 ___, Continued

b.

Return on Stockholders' Equity

Year

Return on Stockholders' Equity = ______________________

____

20Y8: ______________________

____

20Y7: ______________________

____

20Y6: ______________________

____

20Y5: ______________________

____

20Y4: ______________________

____

Name ______________________________

PROBLEM 17-5 ___, Continued

c.

Times Interest Earned

Year

Times Interest Earned = ______________________________

____

20Y8: ______________________________

____

20Y7: ______________________________

____

20Y6: ______________________________

____

20Y5: ______________________________

____

20Y4: ______________________________

____

PROBLEM 17-5 ___, Continued

d.

Ratio of Liabilities to Stockholders' Equity

Year

Ratio of Liabilities to Stockholders' Equity = ______________________________

____

20Y8: ______________________________

____

20Y7: ______________________________

____

20Y6: ______________________________

____

20Y5: ______________________________

____

20Y4: ______________________________

____

Name ______________________________

PROBLEM 17-5 ___, Concluded

2. ____

This Page Not Used.

Name ____________________________

NIKE, INC., PROBLEM

1. a. through m.

	MAY 31, 2016	MAY 31, 2015

NIKE, INC., PROBLEM, Continued

	MAY 31, 2016	MAY 31, 2015

Name ______________________________

NIKE, INC., PROBLEM, Continued

	MAY 31, 2016	MAY 31, 2015

NIKE, INC., PROBLEM, Continued

2. a. through m.

Name ______________________________

NIKE, INC., PROBLEM, Concluded

This Page Not Used.

EXTRA FORMS

JOURNAL

PAGE

	DATE		DESCRIPTION	POST. REF.	DEBIT	CREDIT	
1							1
2							2
3							3
4							4
5							5
6							6
7							7
8							8
9							9
10							10
11							11
12							12
13							13
14							14
15							15
16							16
17							17
18							18
19							19
20							20
21							21
22							22
23							23
24							24
25							25
26							26
27							27
28							28
29							29
30							30
31							31
32							32
33							33
34							34
35							35
36							36

EXTRA FORMS

EXTRA FORMS

EXTRA FORMS

CPSIA information can be obtained
at www.ICGtesting.com
Printed in the USA
FFOW04n0609021217
43855271-42817FF

9 781337 272155